Praise for *Attitude Determines Your Destiny*

Author Bruce Raine has hit a home run with this book! He reinforces the message that it is not what happens to you in life, but how you respond to it and how and why your attitude determines your success in life. If you have ever struggled with setting and achieving goals, this book is for you. My favorite parts of the book are his three pillars for living a successful life: why and how attitude, faith, and goals can transform your life. There are lots of great books written on this subject matter, but this is a keeper for my personal library!

PATRICK SNOW

International Bestselling author of
Creating Your Own Destiny

This is a book written by someone who has obviously climbed the mountain, has done the inner work and therefore writes from a place of heart and wisdom. Bruce Raine's words are filled with practical meaning and ring true because he has traveled the road.

ROBERT DORSETT, PHD

Author of The Grieving Heart

Bruce's writing style is simple and sincere; and extremely impactful.

RANDALL BROAD

Author of It's An Extraordinary Life, Don't Miss It

Bruce Raine delivers! The saying that life is "10% what happens and 90% how you respond to it" has been around forever because it's true. Attitude Determines Your Destiny will inspire the reader to embrace their inner ability to experience a better day every day. Invest the time to read this book and improve your life. You'll be glad you did.

EARL BELL

Author of Winning in Baseball and Business

Attitude Determines Your Destiny is a great investment for anyone desiring a better life.

HC JOE RAYMOND

Author of Embracing Change from the Inside Out

This is a great gift for anyone needing inspiration in life.

AL FOXX

Author of Achieving No Limits

I am convinced that implementing the ideas in this book will improve the way you think and approach life.

KATE PHILLIPS

Author of The Financial Stress Solution

What a powerful message! Truly your attitude will determine how you experience life. Plus you get to choose your attitude.

SHERRI NICKOLS

Author of Sexy and Sparkling After 40

It is amazing that you have everything inside your mind that you need to lead a meaningful life. If you haven't put it into practice yet, this book will propel you forward.

KAREN SZILLOT

Author of Empowering the Children: 12 Universal Values Your Child Must Learn to Succeed in Life

This book is both simple and profound at the same time. It was a pure joy to read.

JUNE KERR

Author of Rabboni, My Love

ATTITUDE DETERMINES YOUR DESTINY

How You Can Live Your Best Life Everyday

Bruce Raine

AVIVA
Publishing
New York

Attitude Determines Your Destiny

Printed in the United States of America
Copyright © 2013 by Bruce Raine

The use of material from this book for educational purposes is ***strongly encouraged***.

Bruce Raine
Seattle Arthro, Inc.
111 Deerwood Road, Suite 200
San Ramon, CA 94583
360-588-4239

www.BruceRaineTaxes.com
www.BruceRaineSpeaker.com

Library of Congress Cataloging-in-Publication Data
Raine, Bruce, 1949-
Attitude Determines Your Destiny / Bruce Raine

ISBN 978-1-938686-37-5

1. Attitude 2. Success 3. Gratitude
I. Title

Published by AVIVA Publishing, Lake Placid, New York.
www.avivapubs.com

For additional copies go to Amazon.com

For large purchases at a discount visit: www.BruceRaineSpeaker.com

DEDICATION

To the people who inspired me to write this book:

The men and women of the military: You risk your lives and sacrifice so much so that we can live in peace. Also, to your families who live without you for long periods of time and then must adjust when you come home.

Lauren, my daughter: I love you more than you will ever know. I hope that you will find peace and contentment in life.

Merle and Kitty Gipson from Shell, Wyoming: You taught me the practice of morning devotions. These morning exercises have changed my life in an incredible way.

Toastmasters: You showed me how to use a talent that I did not know I possessed. You continue to provide me with motivation and joy.

OTHER BOOKS BY BRUCE RAINE:

Achieving Financial Freedom
Attitude Determines Destiny
Attitude Determines Your Destiny
Income Tax Issues for Small Businesses and Self-Employed Individuals

ACKNOWLEDGEMENTS

Who I am today is the result of the effort and influence of many people. I want to thank each one of you for helping me develop as a better human being:

Robert Allen	Sheila (Hittle) Gustafson
Kathy Baird	Stephanie Hankey
Melody Beattie	Marl Victor Hansen
Claudia Black	Napoleon Hill
John Bradshaw	Bill Hybels
Jack Canfield	Susan Jeffers
Dale Carnegie	Alan Johnson
Jesus Christ	Leonard Johnson
Henry Cloud	Vernon Kam
Roberto Dorsetti	Ron Larson
Sir Francis Drake	Albert Levy
Wayne Dyer	Malcolm Maltz
Wyatt Earp	Dick Matthews
Kathy Ewen	John Maxwell
Victor Frankl	James Morton

Elizabeth Murphy	Robert Schuller
Earl Nightingale	Allen Stockall
Joel Osteen	Terry Slotemaker
Norman Vincent Peale	Patrick Snow
David Pirrone	Angela Swanson
John Powell	John Townsend
Anthony Robbins	Brian Tracy
Jim Rohn	Ron Wayne
Bruce Rolfe	John Westfall
Don Miguel Ruiz	Michelle Westford
Bertilla Sampson	Carla Woods
Lauren Sampson	Zig Ziglar

TABLE OF CONTENTS

Thanks	9
Introduction	13

SECTION ONE: GETTING STARTED

Ch 1: Why Change?	23
Ch 2: What Are Your Values?	49
Ch 3: Do You Have Goals?	69
Ch 4: Setting Goals	93

SECTION TWO: LOOKING AT YOUR LIFE

Ch 5: Body-Mind-Spirit Triangle	119
Ch 6: Body = Health and Energy	141
Ch 7: Mind = Knowledge, Discipline, & Wisdom	159
Ch 8: Spirit = Belief, Faith, Confidence, & Inspiration	181

SECTION THREE: LEARNING NEW HABITS

Ch 9: Rocks to Diamonds Cycle	201
Ch 10: Rocks = Our Potential	209
Ch 11: Effort = Using Our Potential	227
Ch 12: Result = Benefit of Our Effort	255
Ch 13: Belief = Changed by Result	271

SECTION FOUR: CHANGING YOUR LIFE

Ch 14: Yes We Can! — 293
Ch 15: Let's Go! — 321
Appendix A: The Three Pillars of a Successful Life — 329
Appendix B: The Only Laws We Need — 331
About the Author — 333

INTRODUCTION

Welcome to *Attitude Determines Your Destiny*. This book is based upon my life experiences and research from the past thirty years as I followed my path of personal growth.

This is for those who would like to enjoy a happier life. My hope is that this book will be particularly helpful for anyone who is currently dissatisfied with life and wants a life that offers more.

You can improve by reading the book, doing the exercises, and growing in the process. Remember you can also improve your life by paying it forward and helping someone else who could use a hand.

I would love to hear your story. My mailing address is:

Bruce Raine
Seattle Arthro, Inc.
111 Deerwood Road, Suite 200
San Ramon, CA 94583

I am also available for seminars and workshops based on this book's lessons. If you or your group would like to sponsor one, please contact me at www.BruceRaineSpeaker.com

My mission statement is, "I will teach people how to change their lives dramatically." This goal comes from the struggles of my own life and the desire to help others to have a better life.

Thank you for your time and effort. I hope that this book helps you, and I hope that your experience and your efforts can help others in the future.

PURPOSE OF THE BOOK

You have great potential. You have treasures hidden inside. They were there before you were born, but they may have been buried under your life experiences. I want to help you discover and develop those treasures within and experience peace and joy and fulfillment in life.

This book is for anyone who wants to get more out of life. Whoever you are and whatever your circumstances, you can make your life wonderful. It doesn't matter what your current circumstances might be, even if you're:

- ☑ Feeling unfulfilled
- ☑ Divorced
- ☑ Widowed

INTRODUCTION

- ☑ Depressed
- ☑ Suffering from PTSD
- ☑ Contemplating suicide
- ☑ Suffering from addiction
- ☑ Feeling unloved, worthless, insignificant
- ☑ Unemployed
- ☑ Feeling life has no meaning

No one's life should be wasted. I believe that you were created to have a wonderful life filled with purpose and meaning. If you don't believe in God, don't let that be a stumbling block. The techniques in this book will work for you no matter what you believe.

What is your purpose? I don't know. Only you can know that. Through prayer, meditation, introspection, and searching, you can find it, even if it takes years. It is never too late. What would be better, to discover those gifts now or to never find them at all?

Purpose doesn't mean that we have to go out and save the world. *Having purpose simply means doing what you were designed to do.* You will know your purpose when you do what truly makes you feel fulfilled and when you use your gifts and talents.

There once was a farmer who lived in the Midwest. For years he was poor because he only grew enough to feed himself and a little extra to sell. One day a geologist came by and discovered that the farm was situated on a massive oil deposit. Overnight the man went from poor to rich—or did he? In reality, he was always rich; he just hadn't discovered what he already possessed. You may be like that with your gifts and talents. You may not have known what they were or that you had them because you hadn't discovered and developed them.

You have the potential to live a meaningful life. You need to do two things to get there:

1. You must *discover* your gifts and talents
2. You must *develop* your gifts and talents

You are responsible for how you live your live. Like the farmer, you can live a life of poverty (one without purpose or meaning) or you can live a life of riches (one filled with purpose and meaning). It is up to you. You have the resources you need. But like the farmer he had to discover the oil under his farm and then develop it. Oil is not much good in the ground.

I wrote this book to be a simple guide. I hope that it encourages you on your journey of personal growth. I also hope that it helps you fulfill the dreams that you have but were too afraid to work toward. Life can only get better if you work at personal growth.

INTRODUCTION

Nothing I say or do and nothing I write can ever change your life. Only you can do that. If you act on what is in this book, I believe with all my heart that your life will change for the better.

HOW DO YOU SPEND YOUR ENERGY?

I recently had some discussions with a management team dealing with employees with poor attitudes. They described how the employees had put so little energy into what they were supposed to do yet they spent so much energy getting around the rules. The team explained that if these people spent their energy trying to do their jobs as well as they could, they would make the workday a better experience for themselves and for everyone around them.

Your attitude affects not only you, but also those around you—your spouse or partner, family members, friends, co-workers, clerks in stores, waitresses, and others. *The good news is that you get to choose your attitude.* You don't inherit it from your parents and or get stuck with it from childhood. You can choose your attitude for each day and for each situation. You can choose the attitude that will give you the greatest satisfaction in life. The best one will contribute greater enjoyment to those around you also.

I'm not saying that you should choose a selfish attitude and try to make only yourself happy. This is short-sighted and leads to a great deal of unhappiness down the road. Instead, you can choose an *Attitude of Gratitude* and look for things to be thankful for in your life. Adopting this attitude will eliminate many of the small problems that you encounter daily. Not adopting this attitude means that you will spend a great deal of energy overcoming minor difficulties.

It is a simple choice that you get to make every day in every situation.

HOW TO GET THE MOST OUT OF THIS BOOK

In order to get the most out of this book, experience it, absorb it, and then *take action*. You'll realize the effort has been worthwhile when you see the benefits you can receive. Consider the following:

1. Look at what's not working for you and let that motivate you to apply the information in this book to those problem areas.

2. Read one chapter each day, preferably when you are the most alert and rested. Pick the time of day when you're at your best.

3. Read each chapter slowly and take notes or underline the parts that are significant to you. Reread a chapter before going on if you need to fully understand it.

4. Do the exercises diligently. You'll find the greatest opportunities for change in them. Absolutely the best way to do the exercises is by hand writing the answers. It makes a greater impression on your mind and on your heart.
5. Each day, use one of the points from the book.
6. Reread the book every month until you feel that you have a good understanding of the material. Then reread it once a year because as you grow, you'll get something different from the material each time.
7. Keep a journal of how you applied this material and what its effects were. It's amazing how life changes when you become aware. Journaling is one of the best ways to become aware of what you're experiencing.
8. This book is only a beginning. Hopefully you'll continue to grow by reading other books and taking other actions to improve your life. Personal growth should be a life-long process.

USE OF THE WORDS SUCCESS AND HAPPY

Happiness is the progressive realization
Of a worthy goal
—Earl Nightingale

In this book, when I use the word "success" or "successful", I do not refer to material success or fame in today's world. I define success as *"achieving what you were designed to do"*. We all have unique gifts and talents and to discover what they are and then to be using them is true success. When you set goals to use your talents and then work towards achieving them you will find success and happiness.

When I refer to "happy" or "happiness," I mean long term inner peace and contentment. I'm not talking about a momentary feeling of excitement based on current circumstances. The main differences are the time involved and the depth of the feeling. True happiness should last longer than a momentary response to favorable events. Also, true happiness is a deep, heart felt feeling not just a superficial response to something that just happened.

I encourage you to read *"Man's Search for Meaning"* by Victor Frankl. In his book, which is a classic of personal growth, he concludes that to feel happy or successful a person needs to find a sense of meaning or purpose in life.

Whether or not you feel successful or you feel happy is up to you. Your life is in your hands and the outcome of your life will be based upon the decisions that you make. Who you are today is based upon the decisions that you made in the past. But who you will be tomorrow will be based upon the decisions that you make today. You can change the direction of your life by changing the decisions that you make.

Section One:
GETTING STARTED

Chapter One

WHY CHANGE?

Know Thyself

—Plato

The title of this book Attitude Determines Your Destiny is not just a catchy phrase. It is a basic truth of life that can be found in most religions and philosophies in the world. It is a lesson that sounds so simple yet is very profound when you start to live it. This chapter will look at some issues in life and see how you might change your attitude and how your life might improve.

I truly wish that I had realized this wisdom earlier in my life. Knowing that my attitude will determine how I experience each day gives me the power to determine how my day turns out.

WHEN DO YOU LIVE?

> *Learn from yesterday,*
> *Live for today,*
> *Hope for tomorrow.*
> **–Albert Einstein**

You don't know when you're going to die, and you don't get to decide how it will happen.

Unfortunately, you are dying from the day you are born. The question to ask isn't "When am I going to die?" but "How am I going to live before I die?" Remember the saying, "I am not alive if I am not living."

Too many people die with their music still in them. In other words, they fail to live life to the fullest. Whatever you believe about what happens after death, you must live intentionally here on Earth.

To do that, *you must live in the present.* Too many people live in the past or the future and then miss out on the present. They lose out on today. If you aren't doing something today because of what happened to you in the past or something you inherited at birth, then you are living in the past and not the present. Just because something was true in the past and limited you in some way doesn't mean that it has to limit you today.

Maybe you had a bad childhood and find that it limits you today. Why would that be? For example, if your father beat you when you were nine years old, what has that got to do with today? You must learn to leave the past behind because its history and you can't do anything about it. *You only have the power to change the present.* You can't change the beating you received or the feelings you felt then, but you can change the way it affects you today.

Likewise, you can't live in the future, giving up today for tomorrow. When you do, you lose today. Some people who are unhappy today feel that they will be happy when an event happens in the future. For example, consider marriage. Frank who is single is unhappy because he's single. He laments that he'll be happy only when he's married. Years later, he marries Becky, but he's still unhappy and laments that he'll only be happy when he gets divorced. People who think like this never live in the present, only in the future. They give away today for the belief that they will be happy later. Generally, these people will always be unhappy in their current circumstances, no matter what they may be.

Are you unhappy because your happiness depends on something outside of yourself, on other people or events? You need to learn how to be happy *now*, no matter what you're doing or what's going on in your life. If you're unhappy, *you* can take steps to make yourself happy. The quickest and easiest way is to think of what you're grateful for. No matter what our circumstances, you can always be thankful for something.

PERSONAL GROWTH EXERCISE:

Answer these three questions:

1. What am I grateful for in life today?

_____
_____
_____

2. What am I grateful for in this situation?

_____
_____
_____

3. What am I grateful for with my health?

_____
_____
_____

> **PLEASE, STOP AND COMPLETE THIS WRITTEN EXERCISE BEFORE GOING ON!**
>
> **BE PART OF THE SUCCESSFUL 2 PERCENT AND COMPLETE THE EXERCISE NOW!**

WHY CHANGE?

When I was a young man I didn't think that I needed to change. I felt that I knew everything and that others should change to be more like me or like I thought that they should be. After I got divorced at age 29 I began to see that maybe I wasn't as smart as I had thought. I went into therapy and started reading self improvement books.

I discovered that like everyone I had issues from my childhood that needed to be dealt with or they would affect my future. The more I learned the more that I wanted to learn. I went from childhood issues to personal growth. I wanted to be all that I could be. I felt that I had some great attributes that I wasn't using. Now I am accomplishing much more and am much happier in life. Today I have a philosophy to push myself outside my comfort zone on a regular basis. It is the only way I can grow.

ESCAPE YOUR PAST

The past is behind, learn from it.
The future is ahead, prepare for it.
The present is here, live it.
—Thomas S. Monson

I wasted many years of my life because I lived in the past. I always felt cheated because my family and my childhood weren't happy and fun. How naïve I was to think that everyone had happy childhoods except me! It took years of counseling to get over my past and to start living in the present. I would love to have those years back but they are gone forever. But I can make the most out of the present and the future.

I had a giant "AHA" moment one day during meditation. After a few years of hard work to overcome dwelling on the past, I had an experience that indicated a huge change had occurred. I always felt that I had this large hole in my soul that was preventing me from feeling successful. One day as I was meditating, I physically felt a movement inside, and I felt this hole close. I learned that that hole was the pain of my childhood. It had been the center of my life until that day.

Up to that point, my therapy focused on my past and my problems in childhood. After that day, my therapy and thinking focused on living in the present and planning a better future. The problems that had controlled my life were now nothing more than unhappy memories.

You can overcome your childhood or whatever traumatic events that may have to you. For some it takes years, but that's better than living in the past for your whole life.

How do you overcome your past? As you progress through this book, you'll learn how to live in the present moment. To truly enjoy life, you must live in the present and not the past or the future. You can't change the past, and you have no idea what the future holds, but in the present, you have the power to make choices and be the person you want to be.

One of the greatest problems that I ever faced was *"negative self-talk"*. We all have self-talk; it is the little voices in our heads usually repeating the words of a parent or grandparent from childhood. If your parents gave you negative messages, then you probably have those negative messages inside of you in the form of negative self-talk. I can remember that I had horrible messages when I was in my teens and twenties.

One day I was walking towards my condo. It was a beautiful, sunny spring day in California. The trees were in bloom and the air carried a wonderful aroma of new life. I was in a fabulous mood because I love spring and I was having a great day. As I walked past a cross walk, I saw some children on their way home from school. I instantly became very depressed and felt miserable for the rest of the day. I couldn't think of what happened until a few days later. Seeing those kids upset me because I remembered the pain I felt at that age.

Unfortunately this happened a lot before I ever discovered what was happening. It took some time before I was able to overcome it. I remember the day it left, what a glorious day. Then I was able to go in and write new self-talk but this time *"positive self-talk"*. I use self-talk and affirmations every day to program the good stuff into my mind.

PERSONAL GROWTH EXERCISE:

You become what you think about most of the time.

—Earl Nightingale

Here is a simple but powerful exercise that will help you overcome past hurts. Before moving on, take time to come up with some specific hurts you've experienced. Hold those in your mind as you work through the exercise.

Positive affirmations are a repetition of positive statements that assist you in changing your beliefs. This exercise addresses the source of the old beliefs and uses positive affirmations to create new beliefs that will be more beneficial.

Use the form on the following page to write down your affirmations. Use the space below each heading to write down what your parents taught you and then write how God made you. Here is what I used—it changed my beliefs about myself in a short time:

God Made Me	My Parents Taught Me
God made me loveable	You are unworthy There is something wrong with you You are not loveable
God made me powerful	You are weak You have no gumption You are not perfect
God made me happy	You can't be happy
God made me filled with Peace and Joy	You are depressed You should commit suicide

Every day, in the morning and evening, read the left column aloud to make this external affirmation an internal belief. This is a quick and powerful way to make changes. Some problems will take more effort to resolve than others, but this is a good first step.

> **PLEASE, STOP AND COMPLETE THIS WRITTEN EXERCISE BEFORE GOING ON!**
>
> **BE PART OF THE SUCCESSFUL 2 PERCENT AND COMPLETE THE EXERCISE NOW!**

I believe that only 2% of the people who read a motivational book actually do the suggested exercises and therefore get the full benefit from the book. Please be part of that 2% and diligently do the exercises as you progress through the book.

God Made Me	My Parents Made Me

Where Do You Live?

Bloom where you are planted
—Mary Engelbreit

Do you say or think things like this:

    I hate getting up in the cold or dark!

    I can't stand this town/city!

    I hate my neighbor!

    I hate my job!

If you live too much in the outside world and have not developed a sense of self, your circumstances will dictate your moods and how you experience each day. You will live only in a reactionary state, where you respond to your circumstances without really thinking rationally first. Your experience of life will be negative.

However, if you have developed a sense of self, the outside world will influence you less. If you have a strong sense of who you are and what you are doing in the world, you will dictate your own moods and how you experience life. You will live proactively and decide how you want to experience each day.

For example, I lived in the state of Washington, north of Seattle. Many people who move here complain about the winters because the days are short and sometimes lack sunshine (some people would consider this an understatement). But some people don't let the gray skies get them down: they put on their raincoats and go about their normal business.

You have to choose your attitude and behaviors each day and not simply react to the circumstances in which you find yourself.

Here is a method that I find helpful. Before I go to bed at night I make a written list of five to ten goals I want to accomplish the following day. When I get up each morning,

I have specific things that I want to do. I try not to let the outside world affect my plan. I dedicate my first hour or two each day to reviewing my goals, physical exercise and inspirational readings. This is a wonderful start to the day!

Depending on what I have planned for the rest of the day, I either get ready to go or continue to work at home. Either way I follow the list I made the night before and try not to get distracted.

I try to start every day like this. It doesn't matter what is going on around me during this period because I'm living in my inner world. It is a time to connect with inner peace and contentment.

The way you experience life is a result of the choices you make

Many people say that they never could do that. It is a choice, and *the way you experience life is a result of the choices you make*. I choose to start my day like this because it engages my body and gets it ready for the day's activity. It also engages my mind because I exercise it when it's most alert. Finally, it engages my Spirit and raises my experience of life to a higher level. I challenge you to try this routine for a month and see how your life changes for the better.

Like many people, I love the long sunny days of summer. But I do not allow the sun or rain or light or dark to determine how I experience my life. If the residents in the Northwest allowed rain to prevent them from doings things, they wouldn't get much done. Yet this area is a center for new businesses and writers who thrive here.

HAVING A PURPOSE

What do you need to do to be fully alive? I don't know. Only you can know what your purpose is. However, I hope that I can help you discover your purpose. The good news is that you have everything inside yourself today that you will need to live a full life. You only need to *discover* what your gifts and talents are and then *develop* them.

Purpose is like a muscle. You need to exercise it to fully develop it. Just like a muscle, your purpose will respond to the amount of activity you engage in and grow accordingly. The meaning in your life will depend on your ability to *discover* your purpose and to *develop* it. You must always look inside to find purpose and meaning in life. Too often society teaches you to look outside yourself for meaning. By looking outside I mean that people turn to food, alcohol, drugs, sex, or other crutches to get meaning. These things simply don't work!

I want to encourage you to live life on purpose, with a purpose. The Greek philosopher Socrates said, "*The unexamined life is not worth living.*" I would say instead, "*The unexam-*

ined life was not really lived." This is true if you merely exist through life but take no positive action to make it better. You are given a limited time on Earth. It may be five years or seventy-five years or one hundred and five years, you don't know. No matter how long, life is a gift, and it is wonderful. You can waste it or have a rich meaningful life. You must decide to live life to the fullest to be happy.

Do you approach life in a passive, reactive way? Do you approach life in a positive or proactive way? Do you think about your life, what it means, and what you want to do with it?

Do you live each day as it comes with little thought about what you want to do? Do you find yourself tired, bored, and unmotivated? These are all signs of an unfulfilled life.

Guess what: it's your life; you can do almost anything that you want with it. If you feel lethargic, you can change that with some physical exercise. If you're bored, you can change that with some mental exercise. If you're unmotivated, you can change that with some Spiritual exercise.

Well, I just described the whole book in one paragraph. I hope that you don't stop reading. I would like to present to you a *simple* plan that anyone (and I mean absolutely anyone) can use to change life from something less than dynamic to a life that is full of energy, meaning, purpose, fulfillment, and personal satisfaction.

Do you take shortcuts in life? For example, you may set as a goal "to be happy." You may believe that happiness is some magic state that you can reach and live in without doing anything. So how do you try to get there? Drugs, alcohol, sex, love, work, money, you name it. But what happens? Do these factors give you lasting happiness? No, they give you only short-term pleasure followed by a period of greater unhappiness than you started with. Life becomes like a roller coaster. The higher the highs, the more excited and happy you are. However, these highs don't last and are followed by lows, so you feel worse. The lows drive you to seek higher highs. This pattern leads to destruction and despair, not lasting happiness. I believe that this is how many addictions begin.

Think of this amazing paradox: if you seek a shortcut to freedom, you will become a slave to that shortcut. But if you exercise self-discipline and restraint, you will be truly free. For example, when Fred was a teenager, he always studied and worked hard at various odd jobs. His friends were always out playing and drinking and doing drugs. At the time he envied them because they were having fun and seemed happy while Fred was stuck working and studying. However, many of his friends ended up addicted to drugs and alcohol, but Fred continued on to college and a successful career. Therefore, their shortcuts to freedom led them into the bondage of addiction, while his sacrifice led him to a life of freedom.

Real lasting happiness comes not from instant gratification; it comes from doing what you were designed to do. *Remember, you were designed for a particular purpose.* Everyone has a unique purpose. It was inside of you the day that you were born. The choices you make in life either lead you closer to that purpose or further away from it. The closer you get to that purpose, the better your life will be and the more fulfilled you will feel. But to find that purpose in life, you must look inside yourself, not outside. You must get in touch with your *body*, your *mind* and your *Spirit* and listen to what they tell you.

DISTRACTIONS

Unfortunately, many people find it very difficult in our present day of instant communications to get the time for introspection. Strangely enough, today's instant communication devices were supposed to save us time and free us up to enjoy our lives. But instead, they often consume our lives. Although we have better communication devices, we seem to have worse personal communication. For example, let's look at the time we spend in a car:

- ☑ It used to be that a person driving in a car had time to be alone and think about their day or their life. Some people experienced stress in the rest of their day but found that they could relax and have solitude in the car.
- ☑ It used to be that two people driving in a car had uninterrupted time to talk with each other. Traveling together was a time to build relationships with spouses, family, or friends.
- ☑ It used to be that a parent would drive the kids and talk with them. This was valuable time together.

Today in cars, I often see the opposite:

- ☑ When people are driving alone, they are often on the cell phone or doing work instead of relaxing and thinking. They often have the radio playing instead of enjoying the solitude.
- ☑ When two people are driving in a car, often the driver (not usually the passenger) is talking on the phone. I don't understand this. I often wonder that if the driver is with friend "A" but talking to friend "B". Then later maybe the driver is with friend "B" but talking to friend "A". Why doesn't this person just talk to who he's with?
- ☑ When parents drive their kids, parents often talk on the phone to a friend or do work while the kids are in the backseat watching movies or television.

I believe that too often our modern communication devices are not used in a healthy way. They are meant to serve us and to make our lives better. Too often they seem to rule our lives and steal the quality without us even thinking about it. For example, if the phone rang right now, would you answer it? You are engaged in reading a book that could change your life, yet you might stop to answer the phone. I sometimes hear people answer the phone and say, "I can't talk now. Can I call you back?"

That's enough whining about cell phones. I think they're amazing devices. I just feel that many misuse them like so many other forms of communication. Television, the Internet, computer games, and other forms of entertainment are making us sedentary, solitary people when what we really need is to be more active and more involved in relationships.

It only takes a little time and effort each day to make your life come alive. The secret is to take a little time every day for *you* because you deserve it. You really deserve to have a wonderful life. But you must work to create it for yourself. No one can give it too you.

To illustrate how you can take time to make your life richer, look at part of a short story by Leo Tolstoy. The title of the story is, "The Three Questions". Think about how these questions and their answers could change your life.

Question 1: What is the most important time?

Now is the most important time. It is the only time in which you have any power. You do not have power in the past or in the future, but you do have power in the present to make choices.

Question 2: Who is the most important person?

The most important person is the person with you *now*. That person is the most important because he or she is the only one you can interact with.

Question 3: What is the most important thing to do?

The most important thing is to do good for the person you are with *now*. To determine how you can serve that person and to take specific actions to do good for that person is the greatest act of love.

Just think of how this could change your life. Whatever you are doing, you are focused on the present moment and the person you are with. This will create more meaningful time together and better life experiences. You will have better relationships and will create more good memories of the time you spend together.

Remember the Golden Rule, "*Love Your Neighbor as Yourself.*" This is a very simple statement of how to live your life. But many people only read half of the sentence. They read "*Love Your Neighbor*" and then start thinking that their neighbor is a difficult person to get along with or he doesn't deserve it. But the second half of the quotation must come first. *"Love your neighbor as yourself"* means that you must first love yourself, then and only then can you love your neighbor. How can you give love away to your neighbor when you don't feel love for yourself?

It is so important that you feel good about yourself. Without this basic sense of self esteem you cannot achieve much in your life let alone affect the lives of others. Remember that modeling is one of the ways that you influence people and showing them that you have good self-esteem is a great attribute to model. Good self esteem does not mean "conceit" but simply a healthy love for who you are as a person.

PERSONAL GROWTH EXERCISE:

Here is an exercise that I learned from a friend. He recommends that you do this in the morning to focus on what you need each day.

Answer these three questions:

1. What do I feel?

_____
_____
_____

2. What do I want to feel?

_____

_____

_____

3. How can I create what I want to feel?

_____

_____

_____

I strongly recommend that you take a few minutes and answer these questions. The best way I have found of getting the most out of an exercise like this is to write down the answers. When you write the answers on paper, you also write them in your mind and in our heart.

> **PLEASE, STOP AND COMPLETE THIS WRITTEN EXERCISE BEFORE GOING ON!**
>
> **BE PART OF THE SUCCESSFUL 2 PERCENT AND COMPLETE THE EXERCISE NOW!**

CHANGE CAN BE SCARY... AND WONDERFUL

It isn't what you have or
Who you are or
Where you are or
What you are doing
That makes you happy or unhappy.
It is what you think about it.
—Dale Carnegie

I'm glad that you've decided to change your life and that this book is part of that process. But if you're like many readers, you may not make it to the end of the book. If you commit yourself to completing this book, then I congratulate you. Your life will change because you'll take the lessons from this book (and other books that you read) and develop your own plan for improvement. There is no one perfect plan: read and study different material and then take what works for you from each source to form your own plan.

Change can happen overnight or over a long period of time. Ideally you continue to grow until the day you die. No matter how long it takes, *personal growth can be one of the most powerful forces in life.* Your life will be better for having read this book, especially if you put some of the information into practice.

If you want to make positive changes, you must take *action*. Some advice will not make sense at first or may not seem to bear fruit for a long time, but if you want to change, you will follow it anyway. Consider the following example.

How do flowers grow from seeds?

HUMAN ACTION STEPS

1. You picture what the flowers will look like.
2. You purchase the seeds.
3. You prepare the soil.
4. You plant the seeds.
5. You water the seeds.
6. You weed the garden.

Steps 1 through 6 give you no immediate feedback.

NATURAL ACTIONS AND RESULTS

7. Seeds sprout in seven to ten days.
8. Flowers bloom in thirty to forty-five days.
9. Once the flowers bloom, they just keep coming.

Life is similar. If you want a wonderful life, you need good self-discipline and preparation. You may need to work for a long time even when you receive no visible results. Then all of a sudden, life will bloom, and it will be wonderful.

To have a successful life, you need to work on it like you do on the garden. You begin by picturing what you want your life to look like. Then you take the necessary preparatory steps to lay the foundation for your life: you set goals to achieve your dreams. You practice self-discipline as you strive toward your goals when you receive no immediate positive results. Once you have set a solid foundation for life, you will continue to receive positive results for a long time. The earlier in life you begin this work, the more time you will have to reap the benefits. But it is never too late to begin.

SUMMARY

I don't want to get to the end of my life and
Find out that I just lived
The length of it;
I want to have lived
The width of it as well
—Diane Ackerman

One of the greatest lessons that I ever learned is that my attitude will determine how I experience each day and ultimately my whole life. The fact that I get to choose my attitude each day means that I can determine what my life will look like.

Another great lesson was to live in the present. For many years I lived in the past and harbored anger and resentment for what had happened in my childhood. I was an adult but felt like a poor helpless child. I acted like a powerless victim. Now that I live in the present I feel free and more powerful.

You can accomplish a great deal by knowing what your purpose is in life. Once you know what you want, you can set goals to obtain it, and most importantly, take action to achieve those goals. We will look at goal setting later.

Chapter Two

WHAT ARE YOUR VALUES?

Who are you when no one is looking?

-Bill Hybels

A subject that does not seem to be very popular today is the question of personal values. Values seem so old fashion and restrictive. Many people feel that they don't allow them to be free.

You have values that you use daily to make decisions. Where did your values come from? Since many people don't actively choose their values, they are using values that family, friends or our society thrust upon them.

I believe that it is extremely important to decide for yourself what your values are and how you choose to live your life.

DO YOU KNOW YOUR VALUES?

It is amazing but most people have never sat down and really thought about what their values are. Few have ever written out their values. But values are the foundation of all of your decisions and actions in life. They determine how you behave in every circumstance in life.

Values are your set of beliefs that reflect your sense of right and wrong or what "ought" to be. Everyone has a core set of beliefs that are used as a guide in making decisions and setting priorities in life. If you know your values it is much easier to make decisions.

For example, one of my core values is to encourage other people. When I see someone sing at church or give a speech at a club or volunteer in the community, I like to go over to that person and tell them that I appreciate what they are doing. It may seem like nothing to me at the time, but for the person receiving the encouragement, it could mean a world of difference.

Another of my values is that I do not lie. This includes little and big lies, they are all the same to me. If I am asked a question I will tell the truth even if the consequences are bad. One time a friend put me in the position that I would have to lie for him. I immediately told him that I could not lie for him and that if he put me in that position he may be sadly disappointed. He understood and changed the situation. He promised to never put me in such a position again.

Values help you whenever you are making decisions – big important ones or small seemingly insignificant ones – and will determine how comfortable you are with the results. How do you make major decisions? Such as:

- What career should I choose?
- Who should I marry?
- Where should I go on vacation?
- Should I check out the porn site my friend told me about?
- Is it okay to lie to not hurt someone?

Your personal values guide you in your decision making all the time

Your personal values guide you in your decision making all the time. While values are fairly stable during a life time, they do change as you mature. However, you can change them dramatically if you want by taking definite action such as you will see later in this chapter.

Another important aspect of your values is that you are passing them on to others who you might influence. Children learn values from parents, teachers and relatives. Members of society learn values from teachers, political leaders, celebrities and people they encounter every day.

Young people learn values from what they see someone do more than what someone says. I have too often seen people tell others one thing and then do the opposite. One day I was driving with a friend and her children. One of the children was caught lying and the mother gave her a scolding in the car. When we got to the movie that we were going to see, the mother proceeded to lie to the ticket seller about the age of the children to save money. What lesson do you think the kids learned that day?

Unfortunately in our world today people often determine what is right or wrong without referring to their own set of values. The four methods I see used instead are:

1. What can I get away with? If I can do it and not get caught, then it doesn't matter.
2. What is legal? I can do anything that is legal, never mind if it is right or wrong.
3. What is everyone else doing? Everyone else is doing it so why not me?
4. No one gets hurt by it! If I do this the only hurt is to the government or business and neither is a person.

I think that the quotation used at the beginning of the chapter "Who are you when no one is looking?" by Bill Hybels

WHAT ARE YOUR VALUES?

sums up values perfectly. When no one is looking at you, what will you do? Will you do the thing that you know is right according to your values or what you can get away with? In today's world where there are security cameras all over the place, you are not as alone as you might think.

Values are choices that you make yourself. For example, are you going to tell a lie? Will you tell a little white lie? Will you lie to save money? No one starts out to be a liar. They start telling little lies and keep doing it until there is a major problem in their life.

As an accountant, I used to go to seminars about fraud and embezzlement as part of my job. Often there was a speaker who had been in prison and could talk with authority on these subjects. Every one of them said the same thing when asked how they got there. They started out doing small things that were wrong. They benefited and didn't get in trouble. Then, they went a little bigger and bigger until finally they were caught. They all said that they felt that they were invincible and would always get away with it.

Let's look at some key values:

1) HONESTY:

I don't think that there is a more important value than honesty. Without honesty nothing you say or do will be believed or trusted by those who know you. It is very easy to spot a dishonest person in almost any walk of life.

I learned honesty as a young boy. My father was a strict disciplinarian. Whenever my brother or I lied he would always find out and the punishment was way worse than the consequences of telling the truth. I learned early to tell the truth and suffer whatever consequences might come my way.

Later in life I saw that lying and then covering it up is one of the worst things you can do. I had a friend who lied but then lied to cover up the first lie. He got in much more trouble by trying to cover up his first lie.

2) PERSEVERANCE:

The ability to continue to work for what you want in the face of great obstacles is a quality of winners. Too often people will quit before they are successful but they often are very close to success but just stop short.

When I was in high school some members of the football team approached me to play football. At 6'2" I was one of the bigger kids in school. I tried out but wasn't picked to play the first game. I spoke with my friend who was trying out also. I asked him

"How long are you going to stick around?"

"I am going to keep trying until I make it!" he said.

I quit and he stayed. Guess who got to play football and guess who never played football again. Perseverance or persistence is a key value to possess. I learned it from that football experience.

> *In the confrontation between*
> *the stream and the rock,*
> *The stream always wins,*
> *Not through strength*
> *But by perseverance*
> **-H. Jackson Brown**

4) PRIDE:

Being proud of everything you do is an important value. Whether I am taking out the garbage or giving a presentation to the president of a company, I do the absolutely best job I can do. I do it because I always want to do my best. Another motivation might be that you never know who is watching you do something.

Often people get jobs because someone was impressed with their work in one area of life and assumed that they would be as conscientious in another job. On the other hand some people take it easy when the boss is not watching and end up getting fired. Even though the boss wasn't watching, he did know what was going on.

5) CONFIDENCE:

Self-confidence and self-esteem are closely related. I define self-esteem as "feeling good about yourself when you are alone" and self-confidence as "feeling good about yourself when you are around other people". This may be splitting hairs but I think we can make this distinction.

In my early life I had little self-esteem and no self-confidence. However, through public speaking I gained self-confidence in front of groups of people. That led to self-confidence in smaller groups of people. But self-esteem was much harder to develop because it was internal and required a lot more work and time. I could "fool" other people but not myself. But I eventually developed self-esteem and am so happy I did.

I view self-confidence like jet fuel. Without it you aren't going far but with it you can go anywhere and much faster than you might have thought.

6) KINDNESS:

Giving to others for no reason is a great benefit for both people. When you give to someone who cannot pay you back it has a reward that is impossible to measure. Almost everyone likes to give to others in some way.

WHAT ARE YOUR VALUES?

I learned this in boy scouts as a kid. We were always supposed to do our good deed for the day. When I saw the responses to my good deeds I felt great. I knew the other person did also. Being kind to people is very easy but can make a huge difference in their day.

You never know when the other person is having a horrible day and your little act of kindness might make a world of difference to that person that day. A simple smile and a friendly "Hello" can make a big difference in someone's day.

7) COMMITMENT:

When you undertake something in life it is important to be 100% committed to it. I know that every job I take on I either commit to it completely or I don't take it on. When I do volunteer work I do it just like I was getting paid a million dollars to work there. That way I do my best at everything that I do.

Sometimes this is called ownership. If you do every job like you were working for yourself and only you benefited from the results, it would change how you looked at the job. The results would be that you did much better work and also that you felt much better about it.

In relationships I have not had that same level of commitment and it shows with the lack of success I have had in marriage. My only advice is to be 100% committed or don't get involved. There is no way to be partially committed in a relationship and to have a successful relationship. Being partially committed is like being partially pregnant – you either are or you aren't!

This is the problem with conditional love. It means that you are not 100% committed. Instead you are committed as long as things are going the way that you want. As soon as they change then you are gone. When you look at couples who have been married for decades you find people that stay no matter what happens in their marriage.

8) FORGIVENESS:

Many people have difficulty with this because they have it backwards. They don't want to forgive the other person and let him off the hook after what that person did. However, not forgiving doesn't hurt that other person nearly as much as you. Once you forgive that other person (who may not even know that you are upset), you are free and experience a great lightness from having that burden taken from you.

I once heard someone say that not forgiving is like taking poison and then waiting for that the person to die.

9) CONSISTENCY:

Being consistent is a value that makes you more reliable. If you are not consistent in your behavior and who you are, then people will not know what to expect from you. If you work hard today and not tomorrow or if you are honest today and not tomorrow, how can someone know what to expect of you the next day?

I had students who would do great work one day and bad work another day. It was hard for me to judge if they were a good student or not because of the variety of performance. They might have been a smart student with poor work habits or a lot of distractions. On the other hand, they may just not have cared about their studies. I couldn't tell from the results.

10) GRATITUDE:

I think that being grateful for what you have is a value that will yield huge rewards in terms of peace and contentment in your life. Everyone sees life through some type of filter. To be grateful means looking for what to appreciate in every situation. Developing an *"Attitude of Gratitude"* is one of the keys to a happier life.

I started this a number of years ago and it changed my outlook on life tremendously. I used to be a negative person and always saw what was wrong in a given situation. Then a friend taught me to say grace before meals. He said that you simply state what you are thankful for at that moment. You don't whine or complain you just say what it is you are grateful for. That helped me to always look for the good in any person or situation. You can always find the good or bad in a person or situation. Why not look for the good? It will lift your spirits every time!

11) PATIENCE:

This is a virtue that will not only provide benefits for others but also yourself, probably more than others. Being patience means being at peace when things are not happening on the time schedule that you want them to happen. You may be upset at the doctor who is keeping you waiting. Whose problem is that? The doctor is not upset like you are.

I used to go to the doctor and everyone complained that he always made you wait from 30 to 60 minutes. Many people would go there knowing this and sit the whole time fuming. They would look at their watch to know just how upset to be. The longer the wait the more upset they would become.

I never understood that kind of behavior. I never wore a watch so I didn't know to get upset. I also took a book with me and sat and read. The doctor was always ready for me before I was ready for him.

12) BALANCE:

I am at heart a type "A" personality, you know: workaholic. But I learned after a burnout in my late twenties that I couldn't do everything and I certainly couldn't do everything perfectly (I was also a perfectionist, not a good combination). After that I started dividing my time into work and relaxation. I didn't allow the two to interfere with each other. When I worked, I was 100% devoted to what I was doing. When I relaxed, I was 100% devoted to relaxing. To this day that has been a great way to avoid stress in my life. It is better to avoid stress than deal with it.

13) HOPE:

How can a person look forward to tomorrow without hope. No matter how bad your current circumstances, life will be better in the future. Life has seasons and none of them last forever. When things are good, enjoy them. When things are bad, keep pushing ahead because your circumstances will change and get better.

Having hope is not completely outside your ability to influence. You can change your attitude towards some situation. You may not be able to control the circumstances in your life but you can control how you react to them. Using that "*Attitude of Gratitude*" will help the way you see situations in life.

HOW TO DEFINE YOUR PERSONAL VALUES

Have you ever taken time out to consider what your values are? Which ones influence you the most in your day to day life?

I would recommend that you take time out to think about your values. Consider whether you are happy with your existing values. Do they truly represent who you are, or are they a set of values that you adopted from someone in your life like your parents? Do you think that it might be a good idea to change some to more suitably reflect who you are today? While most values won't change much during your life; others may change dramatically as you progress and change.

Consider the types of personal values that many people consider to be worthy. Find a list of values and then identify which ones you identify with strongly.

Who is your hero in life? What values did that person possess? Look at those values and see which ones you would like to adopt for yourself.

Clarify your most significant values. This is an important exercise that causes you to focus on the values that matter the very most to you. Once you are more aware of your most significant values, you will be able to use these top values to guide your choices and decisions in life.

Implement your values into your life. It is important to know what values define you. But actually putting them into practice can be another story. Once you have identified your personal values, the real challenge is to live your life by these values. This may necessitate changes in the way that you approach different situations and how you view what happens in your life. This might mean overcoming old habits and adopting new habits.

PERSONAL GROWTH EXERCISE:

Here are a few simple exercises that will help you in identifying your values:

Identify 5 times that you felt extremely happy:

1. _____
2. _____
3. _____
4. _____
5. _____

Identify 5 times that you felt exceptionally proud:

1. _____
2. _____
3. _____
4. _____
5. _____

Identify 5 times that you felt that you had achieved something very special:

1. _____
2. _____
3. _____
4. _____
5. _____

Identify 5 times that you felt intensely loved:

1. _____
2. _____
3. _____
4. _____
5. _____

For each of these situations above, what were the underlying values that gave you those feelings? These should be a good indicator of what your values are.

PERSONAL GROWTH EXERCISE:

Find a list of personal values. Maybe go onto the internet and search for a list of personal values. From that list, make

WHAT ARE YOUR VALUES?

a list of the top 10 values that you identify as yours. That means that they are ones that you either possess now or would like to possess in the future.

1. _____
2. _____
3. _____
4. _____
5. _____
6. _____
7. _____
8. _____
9. _____
10. _____

From the list of your top 10 values, make a list of the most important 5 values:

1. _____
2. _____
3. _____
4. _____
5. _____

Next from the list of your top 5 values, choose the most important 2 values:

1. _____
2. _____

Finally, from the list of your top 2 values, select the one most important value:

1. _____

> **PLEASE, STOP AND COMPLETE THIS WRITTEN EXERCISE BEFORE GOING ON!**
>
> **BE PART OF THE SUCCESSFUL 2 PERCENT AND COMPLETE THE EXERCISE NOW!**

When I did this exercise, I came out with "attitude" as my most important value. Attitude is what determines how someone experience the world around them and how other people view them. I had a negative attitude. I had a victim attitude. These were not serving me well.

While I identified a lot of positive values I thought that I possessed, attitude is one that I hadn't recognized as being so important. That is one of the reasons I started writing books. I wanted to understand attitude better and change my attitude. Because of all the personal growth that I have done, I am happy to report that my attitude is wonderful today. I believe that my change in attitude has made a huge difference in my life.

This exercise is not just a once in a lifetime experience. I would recommend that you review this at least annually to see if your values are shifting or if you want to adopt some different values that fit your current life situation.

SUMMARY

Values define who you are and how you act. There are lots of values but it is important to know what your values are and to use them in any given situation. In the chapter I listed some common values and the role they played in my life.

This was certainly not meant to be anything more than a sample of how you might look at values. It is important to know your values before you start setting goals and working towards a better future.

Chapter Three

DO YOU HAVE GOALS?

*Set your mind on a definite goal and
Observe how quickly the world
Stands aside to let you pass.*
—Napoleon Hill

Goals have changed my life in incredible ways. At various crossroads in my life, I heard a talk on goals and was off on a new adventure. At first the talk seemed boring because I thought that I knew all about setting goals. But hearing that message inspired me to act and that revitalized my life.

The most dramatic time was just after I got divorced at age 28. I truly thought that my life was over. However, I heard a talk about goals and went home and did the simple things that the speaker said. My life immediately took off in an amazing and unexpected direction. It has been one of the most incredible journeys that I have experienced.

GOALS ARE THE CATALYST OF LIFE

Where are you going?

Where do you want to go?

Many people are unable to answer these questions because they've never thought about them. They get up and go about their lives like they have no choice. They just float down the river of life and go wherever the current takes them. That will not get you where you want to go, assuming you even know where that is.

Many people don't have clear lifetime goals. This may be hard to believe, but it's true. Many of my students didn't have any goals beyond graduating and getting whatever job they could get right away. In particular, few people have written goals. I find that putting my goals in writing is very powerful. It makes a deeper impression on my mind and greatly increases the chance that I will accomplish them.

Would you get in your car and start to drive with no end point in mind? Would a pilot fly a plane with no destination in mind? If so, how would the driver or the pilot know when the trip was complete?

Goals are essential to success. People are often afraid to set goals because they think they won't reach them or that if they don't set goals, they can't fail to achieve them. This is not true. It is better to have a high goal and not quite make it than to have no goal at all. Goals are not permanent; they change as you go through life. It's important to set goals and update them periodically—I recommend doing so at least once a year. Some people update their goals monthly, weekly, or even daily.

When I was a university professor, some of my students would not set goals for fear of setting the wrong ones. They felt their lives might be ruined if they didn't set the right goals. An imperfect goal is better than no goal at all. With a goal, we will get moving forward. We may quickly see that we really want to go in another direction, but goals can easily be adjusted. At least we are on our way. Many students started university with one degree or career in mind but changed during their time at college to a different degree program because they had better information than when they started.

Goals have played a major role in my own success. At age eighteen, my only goal was to leave an unhappy home. Going to college was the solution, but I had no idea of where that would lead me except out of where I was. Later, after my divorce in my late twenties, I thought that my life was pretty much over. But after hearing someone talk about goals, I set a goal to get my MBA at a local college. I never got that degree from that college but eventually got my MBA from another college. However, because I had started thinking of what I wanted and where I wanted to go, my life really got kick-started. Once I started the MBA program, I started to think about other things that I wanted in my life.

For example:

Where did I want to live? I discovered that I wanted to live in California and in particular the San Francisco Bay area. I got a job in Hayward, California, and ended up living in the area for twenty-five years.

What did I want to do? I had always felt that my purpose was to teach, so I became a professor and made that my career.

Where did I want to travel? I found that I had many dreams of traveling, and I've since fulfilled many of them. I love England and Australia and have taken two trips to each country. I love tropical islands and I've spent many vacations on islands in the Pacific and the Caribbean. Fortunately, there will always be other exciting places to travel.

What kind of hobbies would I like? I realized that I loved to hike, mountain bike, sail, play golf, explore, travel, and more.

DO YOU HAVE GOALS?

*Once you set goals and get going,
you will just keep expanding your world
and your opportunities*

Once you set goals and get going, you will just keep expanding your world and your opportunities.

Let's look at the Corridor Principle, which is really important as you pursue your goals. If you sit at home waiting until the right opportunity comes along, it may never happen or if it does, you may not recognize it. On the other hand, if you set goals and get started, all kinds of opportunities arise that you would never have seen if you weren't taking action to pursue your goals.

The reason that this is called the Corridor Principle is because setting goals is like a corridor in a large building: when you stand at the end of the corridor, you don't see all the doors down the hall. However, when you start down the corridor you discover that there are many along the way. Each door has another opportunity behind it. If you don't start down the hallway, you will never know that the doors exist. But as you continue down the hallway, you will discover many doors leading to many wonderful opportunities.

Let's do a little review to see where you are right now. There are no right or wrong answers. This is just an exercise to help you become more aware. You must know where you are at present and where you are going.

PERSONAL GROWTH EXERCISE:

Assume that you continue to live your life as you are right now. Answer the following three questions:

1. Where do you think you will be in five years?

_____
_____
_____

2. Where do you think you will be in ten years?

_____
_____
_____

3. Where do you think you will be in twenty years?

_____
_____
_____

Action is very important in life. You can't think your way through these exercises. Doing that is like saying that you want to be physically fit, so you're going to think about exercising. It doesn't do any good. Take time to write down the answers to these three questions before you continue reading further. You will learn a valuable skill to use later in the process.

> **PLEASE, STOP AND COMPLETE THIS WRITTEN EXERCISE BEFORE GOING ON!**
>
> **BE PART OF THE SUCCESSFUL 2 PERCENT AND COMPLETE THE EXERCISE NOW!**

Welcome back! How did you do? Are you happy with what you discovered?

For many people, this is an eye-opening exercise. They find it disturbing, but they can't put their finger on why. If you go through your day-to-day life without thinking of the long term, then this exercise is meant to get you to think long term. *While you must live in the present, the people who succeed are people who plan for the long term.*

Let's say that you have a long-term goal of becoming a doctor. You must keep this goal in mind when you are doing anything. You must constantly ask yourself, "Is this taking me toward my goal?" This is long-term thinking guiding your present activities. For example, becoming a doctor will take years of study, hard work, and sacrifice. You'll have decisions to make every day in the present that will affect that future goal.

You must also think in the short term. To become a doctor, you must take and pass certain courses. If you have the mind-set that this short-term goal is taking you toward your ultimate goal of being a doctor, then it will inspire you to work hard and pass each class.

What if you are not a long-term thinker? Then you'll have much less motivation to pass the class and will have a better chance of dropping out or not doing your best. Long-term goals create energy and excitement that otherwise would be missing from your day-to-day activities. Yes, some people would call this stress, but there are different kinds of stress. Bad stress causes you medical problems and leads you to make bad decisions to escape the stress. However, good stress is a motivator and will propel you toward your goals. The biggest difference is that bad stress is just there and seems to hang around forever. But good stress is there for a time and disappears after you achieve another step toward your long-term goals.

Okay, how are your long-term goals looking? If you think that you don't have any, don't worry about it. You can do an exercise that will help you determine and set specific long-term goals. There is nothing as powerful as a person who is committed to a long-term goal. Goals give you passion and energy. With goals, you will come alive like you have never been before.

PERSONAL GROWTH EXERCISE:

Here is an exercise I always gave my students on the first day of class. While the previous exercise asked, "Where are you headed?" this one asks, "Where do you want to go?" "What is it you want to do with your life?"

For the sake of this exercise assume that there are no restrictions on your life. You have unlimited money, time, knowledge, etc. You want to find out what is deep down inside of you, at the core of who you are as a unique individual.

Answer these three simple questions:

1. Where do you *want* to be five years from now?

_____

_____

_____

2. Where do you *want* to be ten years from now?

_____

_____

_____

3. Where do you *want* to be twenty years from now?

_____

_____

_____

This may sound like the same exercise you just did. However, the previous exercise asked you where you *think* you would end up assuming you make no changes to your life. This one asks where you *want* to be. The first exercise showed you where you were headed. This one shows you where you'd like to go in your life.

> **PLEASE, STOP AND COMPLETE THIS WRITTEN EXERCISE BEFORE GOING ON!**
>
> **BE PART OF THE SUCCESSFUL 2 PERCENT AND COMPLETE THE EXERCISE NOW!**

Just think about what you did today. Did it get you closer to the place that you described in the last exercise?

This exercise is more difficult than the one before it because it requires you to know where you want to go. To do this, you have to think very carefully about your future and decide what you want to do. As I have said, many people are not aware of what they want. You should not feel bad about not having life goals. I believe that many people were never taught to set goals. It is not part of many educational systems, believe it or not. I hope that the result of doing these exercises is that you are now more aware of what you want to do. It will be necessary to redo these exercises many times in the coming years as you grow and change.

DO YOU HAVE GOALS?

The first set of questions really motivated me. When I first asked myself the question, "Where do I think I will be in ten years?" I was twenty-eight years old. My answer to this question was "dead." I seriously believed that if I didn't make significant changes to my life I would be dead (either emotionally or physically) with a decade. Frankly, that didn't appeal to me, so I took action to change my life. Looking back, I truly believe that if I had not taken action, I would have ended up dead by the age of forty.

Even if you get nothing else out of this book, please set goals for your life. Spend some time dreaming about what you want to do. Pray and ask God what He wants you to do. Look at the gifts and talents that He gave you and think about how best to use them. If you use your gifts and talents and do what you were designed to do, success and happiness will follow.

Do you set New Year's resolutions? I never liked making them because they were usually negative. Many people think, "I am fat. I smoke. I drink. I chew my nails," and they make resolutions to stop those bad habits. But it is very difficult to *not* do something. For example, some of us want to diet, so we spend a lot of energy trying *not* to think about food. But, when we are trying to *not* think about food, we think about food. It is better to substitute a new behavior for an old behavior than to try to not do something.

I believe in setting positive goals, such as these: "I weigh 180 pounds on March 31"; "I run fifteen to twenty miles a week by September 30"; "I make five thousand dollars a month by June 30." Then we aim at our goal. If we are positive and clear in stating our goals, we will be more likely to achieve them.

Another important concept is to write your goals down on paper. I know that in today's world of computers this may seem old fashion but it works. When you write your goals by hand you are also writing them in your sub-conscious mind and your heart. The goals then have much greater power. This should be done at least once a year.

Brian Tracy, a wonderful motivational teacher, advocates writing your goals monthly or even daily. It never hurts to write them out more often. He states that the power of written goals is much stronger than unwritten goals. Also, the more frequently you write them, the clearer they will become to you. It is like magic takes over your life and you are propelled forward toward your goals.

Instead of creating New Year's resolutions, I recommend that you spend some time each year reviewing your goals, evaluating how you are progressing, determining if they are still the goals you want, and updating them as you see fit. This will keep you forever going in the direction you want to go. If you never stop to examine your life, how will you ever get to where you want to be, or even know what that place looks like?

ELEMENTS OF A GOOD LIFE

*Good friends, good books,
And a sleepy conscience:
This is the ideal life.*
—Mark Twain

Do you know what a good life looks like for you? Not for me or someone else but for you. What does a good life look like for you? Each of us is different. You must determine what you want in life in order to find true happiness. Although you might share some characteristics with others, your life is and should always be unique. I can't tell you what your life should look like any more than I can tell you what food, clothing, or car you might like or dislike. If anyone ever tries to tell you what you should do in life, you should listen politely and consider what they say but not follow their advice blindly. You must determine what is right for you.

When I was in my last year of high school, I decided to go to university. My teachers and guidance counselors told me that I was wasting my time and would be a "Christmas graduate" (someone who fails out before the first Christmas break). They based their opinions on how I had performed in high school when I was unhappy and had a terrible attitude. However, these were a reflection of my home life that was not very rosy and had nothing to do with my potential or personal desire to succeed.

My primary goal in going to college was to leave my unhappy home. I went to college and almost proved them right, but I got by and received my degree in three years. My attitude had not improved a whole lot, but it was getting better. Then in my late twenties, I got divorced, and I was forced to really look at my life for the first time. That is when I really started to take responsibility for my own life.

You must not be discouraged by anything that people say to you or about you. I proved I wasn't a Christmas graduate. My teachers could only see part of me, the exterior part that was heavily influenced by my dysfunctional family. They couldn't see what was inside me, what would drive me to do better than I had done in high school. My teenage years were the worst years of my life, so my teachers saw me at my worst.

What are the elements of a good life? The following are some ideas. You must determine what is best for you. All the bullet points below are to a large extent interdependent. In other words, you won't be as successful in life if you just have some elements and not the others. You must have a healthy balance.

Primary

- Relationship with God
- Relationship with self
- Relationships with people
- Health

Secondary

- Fulfilling career
- Balanced personal finances
- Satisfying hobbies
- A role in your community

The priority of these will change as you go through life. Today health may mean one thing, but in five or ten years, it may mean something different. A relationship with God will mean one thing in your twenties and something different in your fifties. When you are young, you can't conceive of ever being old. Life expectancies are rising all the time, and most of you will live into your seventies and eighties, and some of you will reach your nineties and even over one hundred. The foundation you set today is not just for today. It is for a long time into the future.

You must be sure that you understand what "successful life" means. This does not mean that you become a millionaire or climb Mount Everest. *A successful life means that you achieved what you were designed to do.* Maybe you were meant to be a truck driver and travel the country; then that is a successful life. Maybe you were meant to have a family and raise children; then that is a successful life for you. For me, it was being a professor, so I feel that I have had a successful life, so far. Success can only be measured by the standard you set for yourself.

> Success can only be measured by the standard you set for yourself

GOAL-SETTING STRATEGIES

*The Best Time to Set Goals Was Yesterday,
The Second Best Time Is Now*
—Unknown

There are many different ways to set goals. You should pick a way that feels comfortable to you and use it. Goal setting is a simple process, but it requires that you know yourself, which makes it much more complex.

Here are some simple strategies for setting goals:

STRATEGY 1

Ask your parents, friends, partner, teachers, or others what you should do. This method assumes that these people know you and have your best interest at heart. If you ask an accountant what you should do for a career and he says to become an accountant, it may not be solid advice. This strategy may not provide you with your goals but someone else's, and you can't live your life for someone else.

STRATEGY 2

Look at your past and see what you have done before. Determine what you are good at and what you are not good at. Determine what you like to do and what you don't like to do. Have you ever been so absorbed in an activity that the time passed while you were not aware of anything else? You were in a "zone" where you were completely content and immersed in what you were doing. You should pay attention to these experiences because they tell you something important about yourself.

Using your past experiences, you can pick out a course of action to take in the future. Remember, you can change it along the way if necessary. The weakness in this method is that your past may not have given you broad enough experience to make an informed decision.

However, this strategy may be better than the first strategy because at least it helps you identify what *you* like or you want to do instead of what someone else thinks you should do. Remember that when you set your goals, you are looking for what you were designed to do.

STRATEGY 3

Brainstorm with some friends. Just throw out ideas with no judgment or evaluation of the idea. I would aim at getting at least 100 ideas before you stop and start to evaluate them. Write them all down until you have exhausted your imaginations. Then you can go back and start categorizing them. For example, divide all the ideas into three groups: good ideas, okay ideas, and bad ideas. You'll need to establish some screening criteria to determine what defines each category. The advantage of brainstorming is that you get to consider things that you might not otherwise have even thought about.

STRATEGY 4

Take a talent inventory or aptitude test. These are tests that show what abilities you possess. There are many free tests on the internet. The test might show you something that you didn't know about yourself. You may discover a hidden talent. Caution; you may be good at something but not enjoy doing it.

STRATEGY 5

Hire a life coach or therapist to help you sort out what it is you were designed to do. This may take some time, but the most important thing is not *when* you figure it out but that you do figure it out before you die. It would be a shame if you lived your whole life never knowing what it was that you wanted to do. The right coach or therapist can make a world of difference and save you a lot of time. You need to make sure you are confident that your advisor is competent in helping you discover your talents. This is easier said than done.

STRATEGY 6

Pray and meditate on what it is that you were designed to do. Prayer is asking God for help. Meditating is listening to God for His answer. Whatever your belief is about God, prayer and meditation are powerful.

Remember that God designed you for a special purpose before you were even born. As humans, it is your responsibility to God and to yourself to find out what that purpose is and then to do it.

You need to be patient if you have trouble figuring out your purpose today. Perhaps you are not ready to know it yet. Perhaps you will find your purpose while you are busy learning who you are. It has taken me thirty years to write this book. It is part of my purpose but I was not ready until now.

If you don't believe in God, then try meditation. This simply means sitting with no distractions and thinking about nothing else. You may also wish to think, "If there was a God, what would He want me to do with my life?"

STRATEGY 7

I used this strategy after I retired to give my life new direction. I felt a bit lost because I wasn't living with purpose. I had this gnawing feeling that I wasn't doing what God wanted me to do. I've always been good with the process of goal setting, so I didn't really examine the method I was using as I tried to figure out what my new goals should be.

One day I woke up and realized that I was trying to set my goals backwards. I had been starting with what I wanted to do when I should have been starting with the gifts and talents God had given me and how I should use those to serve God and others. Within a day of this change in thinking, I was able to write down a new personal mission statement and long-term goals. Writing this book was a step toward these new goals.

I'm an energetic person, and after this change, I simply took off. My life was full every day. When I had been thinking about what I wanted to do, I was limiting myself. When I thought about my gifts and talents, my goals became obvious. God made me a teacher; there is no question about that, so I thought being a professor was what I was supposed to do. That's why I felt lost after I retired.

But when I thought about what God wanted me to do, I was energized all over. I realized that the years of teaching at the university were not the end goal He wanted for me.

It was only part of my training to become the teacher of life skills, God's true intention for me. You will never know true inspiration and passion until you do what you know you were designed to do. What could be greater?

Please, before you leave this chapter, do some work to set five-year, ten-year, and twenty-year goals for yourself. Remember that goals are not set in concrete. You should update them at least once a year and see if they need tweaking or a major overhaul.

WHY PEOPLE DON'T SET GOALS

> *You can get whatever you want in life*
> *By helping others get what they want.*
> **—Zig Ziglar**

Believe it or not but setting goals is not part of most individual's education. Most schools and most universities and colleges either don't teach goal setting or don't give it enough emphasis. It is such an important key to success in any area of life that it should be taught and reviewed every year from kindergarten to graduate school in my opinion.

Many others grew up in homes where setting goals was not a common practice and therefore they simply don't see the need. I know in my home I don't remember my parents ever talking about goals. I never saw my father working towards any kind of goals in his life. But somewhere along the way I learned goal setting. I started setting goals as a boy and have been doing it ever since.

Another big reason that people don't have goals is the "fear of failure". It is strange that in a society that places so much emphasis on success that we have a huge fear of failure. Failure is part of everyone's success. If you have never failed, then you are being too conservative and not reaching far enough. Failure can be one of the greatest learning experiences in life. Look at Michael Jordan who readily admits *"I've failed over and over and over again in my life, and that is why I succeed"*. But we don't consider him a failure.

Remember that failure is an event and does not make you a failure. Too often people think that if they failed in one area of life, they are a failure in all areas of life. You are only a failure if you stop and never try again. It is not how many times that you get knocked down; it is how many times to get back up and continue forward. But *if you learn from the failure and press on towards your goals, then it was just a lesson along the way.*

SUMMARY

Setting goals is probably one of the most important ways to succeed in life. People with goals have passion, drive, and focus in their lives. A by-product of living life with specific goals is that you are generally happier. In addition, others enjoy being around you more.

Success is doing what you were designed to do. Unless you're incredibly lucky and stumble into success, setting goals and working toward them is really the only way to a successful life. You may succeed without goals, but just imagine how much more successful you could be with specific goals.

Chapter Four

SETTING GOALS

What you <u>get</u> by achieving your goals
Is not as important as
What you <u>become</u> by achieving your goals
—Zig Ziglar

Become a millionaire
Not for the money
But what it will make of you
—Jim Rohn

Hopefully now you have a better feel for why you should set goals. This chapter will look at the actual process of setting goals. It is not difficult but does take a little introspection and self-analysis.

The better that you know who you are and what you want for your life, the easier you will be able to set goals. It is so important to living a happy life that I strongly recommend that you make goal setting a regular part of your life.

PLANNING YOUR VACATION

Goal setting is intimidating to some people but it is just like planning a vacation. Just think of the steps that you go through to plan a vacation.

First, you would sit down and dream about the places you might like to visit; your relatives, friends, Hawaii, Australia, Europe, Thailand, etc. When you do this you realize that some may be unrealistic but you don't let this hamper your dreams. Where would you like to go if you had all the time and all the money necessary?

Secondly, you would evaluate the choices, weigh the cost and time and importance to you and then pick the place for your vacation. You would probably get a few pictures of that destination and hang in your house. You would start getting more specific about what you could do during your vacation.

Thirdly, you would start planning your trip. You would figure out what needed to be done now, then later when it got closer to your trip and then during your trip. You would plan when you would get transportation arranged, get a new passport, determine the cost of various aspects of the trip, etc.

Fourthly, you would take action to make your trip a reality. You would buy the plane tickets, get the passport, buy the clothes, etc.

Fifthly, since it takes time to get everything together for a big vacation, it can seem overwhelming. This is when some people give up their dream vacation and settle for something easier to do. If you really want to go on this vacation, then you would divide the work up into smaller pieces. Instead of getting overwhelmed, you would do a little each day until it is all done.

Believe it or not, most people would spend more time and effort planning a vacation than planning their entire life. Going on a trip is a big adventure and involves your money and time. People get excited about a trip and get serious about planning it and getting ready to go. Afterwards they make photo albums and review their trip and the things they did.

Shouldn't your life get at least as much attention as a vacation? It has been shown in study after study and by personal experience that taking the time to prepare goals and then pursue them wholeheartedly will make your life much more successful and happy.

PLANNING YOUR LIFE

The good news is that you already know how to set goals for your life because it is the same process as planning on a vacation. If you set the same five steps above for planning a vacation and apply them to setting goals in your life, you will be able to make significant changes in your life.

Here is a five step formula for setting and achieving goals:

STEP # 1 VISUALIZE WHAT YOU WANT

Visualize or dream about what you want. Write down all the ideas that you come up with during this exercise. Be sure not to use any judgment criteria at this stage. Just think as if there are no limits to what you can do. Use the old rule, "If you knew that you couldn't fail, then what would you do?" Brian Tracy, the guru of goals in my eyes, says to use the Magic Wand Principle. Assume that you have a magic want that you can wave and do anything that you want. What would you want to become if there were no limits at all?

You have tremendous potential and may not even realize it. The process of setting goals and then pursuing them will help you to realize and unlock your potential. When you visualize what you want you will start to see the many possibilities in your life. Things that you might have thought were impossible now look possible with the right amount of determination and work towards achieving them.

SETTING GOALS

When you look at people who have accomplished great things you often think that they are lucky or had all the breaks in life. Most people like this are not lucky or have not gotten breaks accidently, they work hard to make these things happen. How do you think Elton John became such a great performer? It was through years of dreaming and setting goals and working hard towards those dreams and goals. Did he have to sacrifice? Yes, it took years of practice to be as good as he is. Was the sacrifice worth it? It would appear that his sacrifice was worth it because he is so successful. He would be the only person to say if he thinks it was worthwhile.

Don't let the fact that you are going to have to work hard discourage you. When you work hard and get little more than a paycheck, it can feel frustrating. However, when you work hard towards your dreams it doesn't seem like work. For example, think of your favorite sport or hobby. Do you consider the effort you put into it work or part of the pleasure of the activity?

When I was a kid I hated to run. Every time I tried to run I got tired and winded quickly. However, I loved playing baseball; from early spring until late fall I played baseball and loved it. I would run hard to catch a ball or run the bases after getting a hit. I never considered it work since it was simply a part of the game I loved.

STEP # 2 SET SPECIFIC GOALS

Get specific by setting goals. After you have visualized the things that you would like to do, you need to evaluate them and determine what you are going to spend you time pursuing. Unfortunately, life is too short to do everything and you don't have the skills to do them all anyway.

It is important to pick goals that fit your purpose in life and your strengths. Although being a great performer like Elton John may appeal to you, do you have the strong desire or skill set to be like him? My desire in life is to teach and help people. My skills are that I am empathetic with people and have the ability to understand where they are and how to get them to where they need to be. I have the ability to speak with confidence to groups of people. I used these strengths to be a professor at a university and now to teach people life skills.

When setting goals, they should be as detailed as possible. The real power in goals comes from seeing them clearly. Here are five techniques that will help you:

Technique # 1

Write your goals down on paper. By this I mean to write them by hand with a pen or pencil, not a computer. The act of writing your goals reinforces them in your sub-conscious mind and your heart as well as on the paper.

SETTING GOALS

I cannot emphasize enough how important it is to write down your goals. It is probably the most important part of the whole goal setting process. When you write down your goals, you obviously have them figured out enough to write them down. Clarity in goals is a critical component. Also, as you write them on a piece of paper, you write them in your subconscious mind. This means that your subconscious mind will be working on your goals even when you are not aware of it.

When you write down your goals they should be stated in the positive. If you want to lose weight you would not set a goal of "I don't want to be fat" or "I want to lose 20 pounds" instead you would write "I weigh 185 pounds on June 30, 20xx". This is positive. New Year's resolutions are usually negative and usually not successful. What are typical New Year's resolutions? Many want to stop bad habits like eating too much, smoking, drinking too much, etc.

Goals should be written in the present tense as if you have already accomplished them. The goal "I weigh 185 pounds on June 30, 20xx" is stated in the present tense as if I had already achieved that goal.

Goals should always have a definite date for accomplishing them. I didn't write that I wanted to weigh 185 pounds because that could mean 20 years from now. I put a specific date when I would weigh that amount.

Goals should be measurable. I want to be skinny or I want to lose some weight are too vague. How would you know if you actually met your goal? "I weigh 185 pounds on June 30, 20xx" is very specific. It would be easy to measure if I achieved my goal or not.

Technique # 2

Prepare a vision board which cements your goals with a strong visual presentation of what you want.

The use of a vision board to "picture" your goals is very powerful. Writing your goals gets them into your subconscious in one form. The vision board gets them into your subconscious in picture form which helps you "see" yourself having achieved the goal. This is particularly important if, like me, you don't really picture things in your mind very well.

I spoke with a friend of mine one day and told him that I wanted to go to Australia on a book tour. I knew that he had been there and asked him how he had arranged it. He told me that he prepared a vision board and put it on his wall. It had pictures of what he wanted to do and see in Australia: the Opera House, the Sydney Harbor Bridge, Great Barrier Reef, Melbourne, Perth, etc. He said every day he looked at his vision board and thought about Australia.

One day while talking to a friend, his friend said, "I am going to Australia next month on a speaking tour, why don't you come along with me?" Amazingly his friend did not know of his dream to go to Australia. This is typical of the kind of things that happen when you use a vision board.

Technique # 3

Make a vision book with pictures, writing, drawings, mementos, etc. Use a scrap book or photo album and fill it with your goals using anything to make a stronger impact on you. This is similar to the vision board but easier to carry around. If you saw the movie *The Last Holiday* with Queen Latifa, you will remember that she used a vision book throughout the movie. In the movie it showed how her life changed dramatically to make her visions come true. The same can happen in your life.

Similar to the vision board, the vision book helps you picture the goals that you have set. One time when my daughter was a little girl I wanted to take her on a special vacation in California. I took a simple photo album and put in pictures of San Francisco, the cable cars, Great America, Disneyland, Knotts Berry Farm and other things that I thought that she would like.

The following summer we took that trip and it was wonderful. I took the photo album and inserted pictures of us doing those things. I put in ticket stubs and flyers and other things indicating that we had done those things. Today that book is a valuable memory of that summer vacation.

Technique # 4

Review your goals daily. I recommend that you put them on 3 x 5 cards and review them first thing in the morning and last thing at night. Also, review them when you can during the day. Put signs on your fridge, computer and mirrors. Write out your goals daily without looking at the list you already made.

Technique # 5

Speaking your goals daily is very powerful also. By this I mean stand in front of a mirror, look yourself in the eye and speak out loud to yourself. Tell yourself with passion and enthusiasm what your goals are and that you are living the life that you dream about. The more emotion that you put with this, the greater will be the impact on your sub-conscious.

STEP # 3 PREPARE PLANS

Set detailed plans for accomplishing your goals. The plan should have three parts to it: One Year Goals, Five Year Goals and Ten Year Goals. Each section should contain detailed objectives with a deadline for each one. The One Year Goals can be broken down further to monthly, weekly and daily goals. I have my goals broken down like that. Every night I review my goals and write down the goals I want to achieve the next day. Obviously they are smaller than the big goals, but they are getting me closer to my big goals.

Let's go back to my goal to weigh 185 pounds on June 30, 20xx. I can dream about it and set that goal. I can write it down and put my picture on a vision board or in a vision book which will all help me picture that goal. But how do I plan to get there? I need to write specific plans of how I am going to achieve my goal.

For example, what am I going to eat to help me get there? Zig Ziglar tells the story of going to the doctor and his doctor told Zig that he needed to lose weight. The doctor said

"I have some good news for you Zig, you can eat anything that you want to eat. Here is the list of what you want to eat."

If you want to change your life by setting goals then you have to change your behaviors to achieve them. Many people want to get better results without changing their behaviors. If you want to be successful you must have success habits. If you have failure habits you will not be successful. If you want to lose weight, you must develop success habits to achieve it.

How am I going to change the way I eat? I am going to eat primarily fruits, vegetables and whole grains. I am going to avoid processed sugar and processed flour (i.e. white sugar and white flour which means all baked goods).

How am I going to change the way I exercise? I am going to walk one hour every day. I am going to walk 500 miles in the next 12 months.

How am I going to change the way I think about food? I tend to be a mindless eater. I can open a bag of chips or nuts and eat the whole thing without thinking about what I am doing. I will buy smaller containers of food and be more conscious when I eat.

The use of a journal is a great way to monitor my progress and inspire me to keep doing the correct things. I keep a health journal beside my computer so that I am reminded to use it daily. It contains my weight each day, the time I ran or walked and the distance I covered. I also put down where I was and anything special about the day.

The advantage of a journal is that it has every day written in it. If you skip a day you see that it is blank and that inspires or reminds you that you need to do something today towards your goal. I cannot stress enough how important it is to develop new, successful habits to replace the old habits that were not working.

STEP # 4 TAKE ACTION!

A goal without action is just a dream that is not going to come true. Procrastination is the biggest problem at this stage. Be sure to take action immediately and don't stop for anything.

Are you a procrastinator? Here are a few quotes about this popular subject:

> *Never put off until tomorrow*
> *What you can do the day after tomorrow*
> **—Mark Twain**

> *Procrastination is the thief of time*
> **—Charles Dickens, David Copperfield**

> *You cannot escape the*
> *responsibility of tomorrow*
> *By evading it today*
> **—Abraham Lincoln**

> *Never put off for tomorrow,*
> *What you can do today*
> **—Thomas Jefferson**

It is amazing how much is written about procrastination. I read the other day that our brains are naturally lazy. They want to reserve their strength for when it is really needed.

Therefore, we are programmed to procrastinate and must overcome the brain's natural tendency to put things off.

The hardest part of doing most things is getting started. The reason so many people fail at being self employed or writing a book is that they don't get started. A common saying of people who want to be writers is:

"I just don't know what to write about. As soon as I figure that out I'll get started."

If you want to be successful you must be able to overcome the inertia that discourages you from starting. That is why there is a date with a goal. Most people do better with a deadline than an open ended goal.

Set some time to work towards your goal. When I was a student I would spend my evenings studying. When I write I write first thing in the morning. I set my alarm for 6:00 am and get up and write for 4 hours. Do I feel like it every day? No, but I find that once I start I get involved and pretty soon the 4 hours are done and I have accomplished way more than I thought that I could that day.

If I truly do not feel like writing, then I do some related task. I look up quotes for my chapters or design a new exercise or research a topic that I need to know about. But I spend my four hours doing something to get me closer to my goal.

You know yourself best (I hope that is a valid assumption). What is the best way for you to accomplish things? If you don't have a good track record of accomplishing things in your life, then research time management skills. It is not difficult to manage time. It is just not desirable for some people. However, just a few small changes in the way that you manage your time can make huge differences in your achievements.

Time management is nothing but self-discipline. Self-discipline is necessary to do what you should do to reach your goals instead of what you want to do. How do you do this? Make reaching your goals extremely important by using the techniques discussed previously. Also, make not reaching your goals very painful because of everything that you will miss. This gives you a carrot (incentive) and stick (punishment) to motivate you towards your goal.

Time management is like a snowball gathering more snow. Once you see how you can improve you will be constantly looking for better ways of doing things and getting more and more productive all the time.

Here is an interesting idea. Do you think that you get improve 1% tomorrow? Probably yes. What about the next day, do you think that you could improve 1% that day? Probably yes. Instead of trying to double your productivity, just try to improve 1% a day which seems fairly easy to do.

Guess what happens after just three months of doing this? You would have double your productivity in that short period of time.

STEP # 5 BE CONSISTENT

Spend at least one hour everyday working towards your goal. You will be amazed by how much you can accomplish in one month or one year when you spend one hour a day working towards your goals.

It has been said that if you spend a mere one hour a day working towards a goal (new language, playing a musical instrument, etc.) that in one year you will be proficient and in three years you will be an expert. Can you find one hour a day to spend working towards your goals? Do you own a television? If you are a typical person who spends 4-6 hours a day watching television (WHY?), then all you have to do is spend one hour less watching television and spend that one hour working towards your goal. Maybe one hour less on the Internet or Facebook could yield the same result. I am sure that no one ever laid on their deathbed and said

"I wish I had watched more television."

Successful people have libraries
The rest have big screen TVs
—Jim Rohn

The other great thing about the one hour a day is that it develops a great habit of working one hour a day on the most important thing in your life: your future! The one hour a day should be the first hour of the day if possible. That makes your future your top priority. Many people waste time doing unimportant things and then have no time left over for themselves.

> *Work hard at your job and*
> *You can make a living.*
> *Work hard on yourself and*
> *You can make a fortune.*
> **—Jim Rohn**

SELF-DISCIPLINE

How badly do you want to achieve your goals and have a better life? Most people want the better life but they don't want to do what it takes to get there.

I want to be skinny but I don't want to diet.

I want to be in shape but I don't want to exercise.

I want a bigger paycheck but I don't want to do anything extra to earn it.

Does it make sense to expect to get something yet not put out any additional effort to get it? You are not going to get skinny unless you eat fewer calories and burn more calories.

You are not going to get fit unless you exercise.

You are not going to get a bigger paycheck unless you improve your value to your company by improving your skills.

Self-discipline is necessary to achieve your goals. Self-discipline is simply you telling yourself what you need to do and when you need to do it. People often don't like being disciplined because they have to do something that they don't want to do. In this case, you want to achieve the results so you just need to tell yourself that you need to do the work that goes into it.

> *Self-discipline is simply you telling yourself what you need to do*

While it sounds tough, it is actually quite easy and gets easier as you develop the good habits necessary to achieve success. People often wonder about how I write. I must admit that at first it was difficult just like any new activity. But, as I got more practiced and knowledgeable about how to write, it became easier and now is very enjoyable. It was just a matter of self-discipline that eventually led to it being a habit.

> *Discipline is the bridge*
> *Between goals and accomplishment*
> **—Jim Rohn**

PERSONAL GROWTH EXERCISE:

Write out at least three goals that you are going to achieve during the next:

1. Five years

_____
_____
_____

2. Ten years

_____
_____
_____

3. Twenty years

_____
_____
_____

It doesn't matter if you're eighteen or eighty; this is an important exercise that will energize your life.

> **PLEASE, STOP AND COMPLETE THIS WRITTEN EXERCISE BEFORE GOING ON!**
>
> **BE PART OF THE SUCCESSFUL 2 PERCENT AND COMPLETE THE EXERCISE NOW!**

MAKE A DRAMATIC CHANGE IN 30 DAYS

How do you feel about goals and about your personal goals? Did you do the exercises in this chapter? If not, why not?

- I don't want to write them down
- I'll do it later
- I kind of know what I want anyway
- I don't have enough time

Whatever your reason, it is an excuse. Next to belief in God, goal setting is probably one of the most important ways to succeed in life.

The best way to start on a new project is to start right now; not tomorrow morning or next week, right now. Try this 30 Day Challenge and you will make great progress towards your goals. Follow it for thirty days, and I *guarantee* that it will change your life.

1. Select one goal from the list in the last exercise of one year goals. You may want to break it down into smaller goals instead of trying for something too big all at once.
2. Then, pick the goal that you believe would make the greatest impact on your life if you were able to achieve it.
3. Write that goal at the top of the next page. Below it, write ten things you can do to accomplish that goal.

4. For the next 30 days, spend at least one hour *every* day working toward this goal. Ignore all other goals for the next thirty days and work on this one exclusively.
5. At the end of the month, look at where you are and compare that to where you were at the beginning. I guarantee that if you follow these instructions; your life will change significantly.

This exercise is very powerful because it demonstrates:

- The power of goals
- Our commitment to our goals
- Our self-discipline
- What we can accomplish in just one hour a day

The one goal that would make the greatest impact on my life:

_____
_____

The ten smaller goals that will get me to my one big goal:

1. _____
2. _____
3. _____
4. _____
5. _____
6. _____

7. _____
8. _____
9. _____
10. _____

Here is an important part of this 30 Day Challenge. You should work at least one hour every day towards your goal. If you do nothing all week and then on Saturday spend 7 hours working towards your goal, it will not work. It is the consistent effort that develops into a success habit. That produces the result but also changes you into a more productive achiever of your goals.

Did you do the goal-setting exercises? If not, I suggest that you stop reading. Proceeding without doing the exercises will mean that you will get less from the following material. It will be like building the second floor of a building before you've finished the first floor. I recommend that you return to the beginning of the chapter and do the exercises. It is important to write them down as instructed.

SUMMARY

Setting goals is probably one of the most important ways to succeed and be happy in life. Earl Nightingale, a very famous motivational author and speaker, even defined success as, "the progressive realization of a worthy goal." That is how important goals are, they define your life and help determine your success.

People with goals have passion, drive, and focus in their lives. A by-product of living life with specific goals is that goal achievers are generally happier people. In addition, others enjoy being around them more.

> *My definition of success is,*
> *"Success is doing what you were*
> *designed to do."*

Unless you're incredibly lucky and stumble into success, setting goals and working toward them is really the only way to a successful life. People may succeed without goals, but just imagine how much more successful they could be with clearly defined goals.

The 30 Day Challenge is a powerful tool for making dramatic changes in your life. The first step is getting started on accomplishing your goal, whether it is large or small. I use the 30 Day Challenge on a regular basis.

Section Two:

LOOKING AT YOUR LIFE

Chapter Five

BODY-MIND-SPIRIT TRIANGLE

*The Strongest Geometric Shape
Is the Triangle*
—Euclid

The way that you look at yourself is important. Too often people see themselves in a negative light or don't even know how to look at themselves.

This chapter will speak to the three important elements of your being: your body, your mind and your Spirit. Each is important to the successful operation of your life. Not one can be ignored or the other two will fail to function properly.

When you get all three working in harmony, you will be riding a wave of success and happiness that can carry you a great distance in your life.

THE THREE FACETS OF YOUR BEING

A person's being can be broken down into three distinct parts: the *body*, the *mind*, and the *Spirit*. While they are three parts, they are interconnected and interdependent; like a musical triad that must be played together to produce a harmonious sound. You must play the three parts like that triad to produce a harmonious life. *When you want to change, you must coordinate the three facets of your being, or you won't be successful.*

Unfortunately, many people don't coordinate the three parts and work on only one. Let's look at a couple of common examples: dieting and quitting smoking. What percentage of people do you think are successful at breaking the two habits of unhealthy eating and smoking? A very low percentage!

Mark Twain once said, "*It's easy to quit smoking. I've done it hundreds of times!*" The same is true with dieting: people try over and over but often end up weighing more than before.

Why do so many people fail at something that seems so important to them and would seem simple to do? Just stop eating so much. Just stop smoking. It's easy! I believe that the main reason so many people fail is that they fail to coordinate their minds, bodies, and Spirits. As illustrated in the following diagram, the three facets are interdependent.

BODY-MIND-SPIRIT TRIANGLE

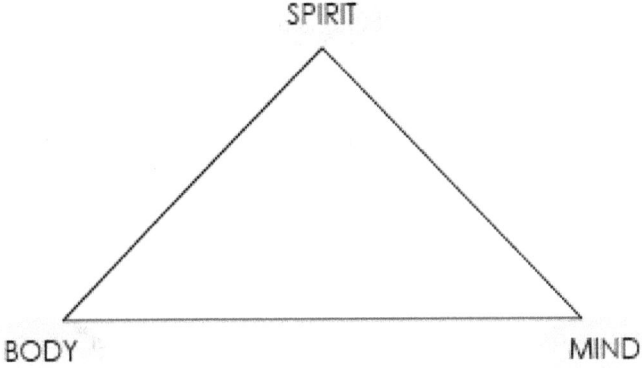

One would think that dieting is primarily a body function. However, if you try to diet without engaging your mind (with knowledge of health and the self-discipline to eat less) and the Spirit (with the belief that the body is a temple of God and the inspiration to be healthy), you will probably fail. The same is true of giving up smoking or just about any other addiction.

Another barrier to changing behavior is the approach taken. You must approach it positively: "I want to be healthy" and not negatively: "I want to stop…" If you believe that you want to be healthy, you have a good chance of success. But if you are only focused on stopping the problem, then you are setting yourself up for failure. You must focus on what you want and not focus on what you don't want. Remember you become what you think about most of the time. If you are thinking about not being fat, you are thinking about being fat and not think about being thin.

If you engage the three elements, you will have fantastic power and a much better chance of success. Let's look again at dieting since it is such a common activity in our country. What does dieting mean to us? Sacrifice? Deprivation? Starvation? For many, dieting is negative and comes with many bad associations. Just think; the word "diet" starts off with the word "die." This is not a good beginning! A better approach to weight management is to set a goal of being healthy. You need to determine a healthy weight range for yourself and work toward that. A common measurement of healthy weight ranges is the Body Mass Index (BMI), which indicates healthy and unhealthy ranges for your height. The BMI can be found and easily calculated on the internet.

The first facet (the body) will engage in eating less, eating better quality food, and getting exercise. Your body knows intuitively what it needs for good health. However, with society's abundance of cheap, unhealthy food and a philosophy that food can be eaten almost everywhere and at any time, it is more difficult to eat in a healthy manner. If you try to be healthy using your body alone, it will be very arduous.

But, if you also engage the second facet (the mind), then your chances of success will be greatly enhanced. For example, you use your mind to research healthy habits and the reasons why you should practice them. Then you will better understand why to be healthy and how to be healthy. That will help you develop stronger self-discipline. Can you resist a rich, gooey chocolate snack? The snack will be easier to resist if you know that it might hurt you than if you feel you should resist simply because you are on a diet.

Finally, if you engage the third facet (the Spirit) and come to believe that God made you to be healthy and created your body as a temple that holds His Spirit, then it will be even easier to do what you need to do to be healthy. God wants you to be happy. Your good health will bring you peace and joy. Good health is the foundation of a good life. It is very difficult to be successful and happy with bad health.

By combining the power of the three facets of your being, you will be better able to accomplish what you want in life. I will use a simple mathematical equation to illustrate the power of the three facets. You might expect that the three facets add together. To show this, I will assign each facet a value of 10. The value of your three facets would then add up to 30:

Body + Mind + Spirit = Power
10 + 10 + 10 = 30

But this is not the case! The three facets instead appear to multiply each other's effects, yielding greater power than simple addition.

For two facets, the relationship looks like this:

Body x Mind = Power
10 x 10 = 100

These facets generate even more power if all three are combined:

Body x Mind x Spirit = Power
10 x 10 x 10 = 1,000

When you try to do something with just one facet of your being, you either don't do as well as you want to or you just don't complete what you want to do. But, if you combine a second element, you do much better than you would by using just one. If you combine all three elements, then you can do almost anything. I believe that if you look into your past success that when you achieved something significant, it was because you combined all three facets of your being.

Sometimes you may feel that you are successful without combining all three elements. I would like to say two things about this assertion:

First, are you sure that you didn't use more of the elements than you thought? Maybe a good athlete attributes her performance only to physical prowess. But did her mind coordinate and direct that ability to a higher power? Did the Spirit give her the faith to do well? Belief that you will do well is an essential element of performing well. *You can raise your level of performance dramatically if you firmly believe that you will do better.*

Second, if you feel you did well and you truly didn't use all three facets of your being, just think about how much greater you could have performed if you did use all three facets.

Before we leave this discussion of the combination of the facets of life, let's look at another example that shows how the facets combine to result in dramatic power. I believe that the facets are not all equal in value. Instead of giving each of the facets a value of 10, I believe that the mind is greater than the body, so it should have a greater value, maybe 100. I further believe that the Spirit is the most powerful of them all and should have an even greater value like 1,000. If you look at the product now, you will see even more power.

Combining the body and mind, you get:

Body x Mind = Power
10 x 100 = 1,000

Combining the body, mind, and Spirit, you get:

Body x Mind x Spirit = Power
10 x 100 x 1,000 = 1,000,000

I believe that this is the case and it demonstrates three important points:

First, the 1,000,000 is so much greater than the 30 at the beginning of this discussion. I believe that this explains why some people perform at a level so much higher than average. Not just a little higher but way, way higher.

Secondly, this illustrates that the Spirit is essential to reaching truly high levels of performance in your life. If you do not believe in God, it is important to believe in some higher power that is inspiring you.

Thirdly, while the Spirit may be the most powerful, I believe that it is dependent on a healthy body and a healthy mind to function properly. I strong Spirit without the healthy body and healthy mind is severely limited in what it can do.

COORDINATING THE THREE FACETS

Next let's look at communication. This is such an important part of success. I am not talking about external communication but internal communication. How do you communicate among the three facets of your being?

BODY

The body's role is the easiest to understand because you are the most familiar with it and use it so often. You communicate by seeing, listening, and speaking. Two are for input and one is for output. I have heard people say that you are supposed to listen and see more than talk because you have two eyes and two ears but only one mouth—you have four channels to receive communication but only one to send communication.

There is a saying that if you're silent, people might think you're a fool, but if you open your mouth and talk, you will remove any doubt!

However, this is all external communication. Internal communication with your body has to do with feeling or sensing what is going on. Some would call this "intuition". How do you know that you are hungry, thirsty, sexually aroused, etc.? You feel those things and you can take action to remedy them.

But at a different level how do you know if your body needs salt or a particular vitamin. You don't usually have that same kind of obvious feeling. Usually you have an unusual craving or desire that leads you to a particular food. That is your body telling you what it needs.

For example, I have always eaten a low salt diet. In fact it has often been salt deficient. There was a period in my life where I would occasionally crave fast food French fries. Since I never ate fast food or much processed food, this seemed very strange to me. But eventually I would go in and get some French fries and the craving would disappear. After a while I realized that this craving was because of a lack of salt. Because I had a small inflow of salt and since I was very physically active I had a large outflow of salt, there was an imbalance.

MIND

The second form of communication happens with your mind. You are probably less familiar with this form. You might believe that thinking is how you communicate with your mind. That is only a small part of the communication. Your mind has two distinct parts, the conscious mind and the subconscious mind. You must communicate with both parts in order to fully use your mind. In my twenties I learned how to communicate with my subconscious mind. This was a very important discovery. You must understand that the subconscious is there and that it is a significant part of your life.

I believe that your subconscious mind has three basic functions:

First it is where you store information like thoughts and memories over the long term. It is also where you go to retrieve your long-term data.

Secondly, it controls your day-to-day activities like walking, running and driving, without you even knowing it. Your subconscious mind is like a computer that has been programmed to perform certain tasks. It will run those programs over and over without changing them. This can be good or bad. If you have good programs, then you will get good results. If you have bad programs, you will get bad results. The good news is that you can reprogram your subconscious mind, but it takes deliberate effort.

God wrote your original programs for your benefit. However, your parents and caregivers changed them before you reached the age of seven. While you were in the womb and as a young child, the events that were occurring in your parents' lives were being communicated to you and absorbed by your subconscious. This influenced your views of what the world is like and what you need to do to survive. Many people don't know what these programs are, but if you ever did something and later wondered why you did it, it was probably coming from your subconscious programming.

For example, when you were learning to drive a car, it seemed difficult and you had to think through each part and concentrate on the task. But now you just drive without giving it much conscious thought. You have moved driving from your conscious mind to your subconscious mind. This is true of anything you do so frequently that it becomes routine. This is how you program or reprogram your mind.

Do you repeat certain ideas to yourself or think recurring thoughts during the day? Many people do. This is called "self-talk." Self-talk is nothing more than thoughts your subconscious mind repeats. These messages are communicated to your conscious mind. They can be either positive or negative.

In my world, negative self-talk came from my father. He taught me that I was worthless by constantly repeating what was wrong with me. Therefore, he reprogrammed my subconscious mind with his negative affirmations.

As an adult, my subconscious, which had dutifully stored these messages, constantly repeated them back to me. They were my daily affirmations. My negative self-talk told me that I was bad at sports and would always be a loser. But I had good athletic ability and picked up sports easily. However, I could never win at sports when I was young. When I played tennis, no matter who I played, I always came in second. I have a lot of natural ability for golf, but again I always came in second. I wasn't competitive in sports because of this.

The subconscious mind is powerful and true to its programs and it can control your life in ways you can't imagine. It's very important that:

- You know what is in your subconscious mind
- You reprogram your subconscious mind to not work against you
- You program your subconscious mind to work for you

As with a computer, you need to know what is in it and to learn how to use the programs appropriately. That means learning about your computer. You need to keep the programs that help you and remove ones that don't.

I had to work hard to reprogram my subconscious mind. The hardest part was removing the negative thoughts. Replacing them with positive thoughts was easier and is an ongoing process getting better and better all the time. Now my subconscious mind works for me instead of against me.

Thirdly, the subconscious mind is where you process problems and find solutions. Much of this will happen when you are asleep. If you have a problem and you think or pray about it just before going to sleep, you will often wake up with the solution and it will be one that your conscious mind was not even considering.

When you dream it is the subconscious mind trying to work out a problem. If you have the same recurring dream, it is because the subconscious is trying to work something out but is having a problem. This is why it is so important to know what your dreams mean.

What is your subconscious mind doing in your life? In the next exercise, take a few minutes to think about how your subconscious mind is working. Does it send positive or negative messages? Is it helping or hindering you? If you have never thought about a subconscious mind, just take some time to meditate on it and see what comes up.

If you have difficulty with this exercise, try thinking of something that you did that made you think afterward, "Why did I do that? I know better" or "I didn't want to do that."

PERSONAL GROWTH EXERCISE:

Write down at least five *negative* messages that your subconscious mind has sent you in your lifetime. Think of situations where you did something and then afterward wondered why you did it and couldn't think of a conscious reason for it.

1. _____
   _____
2. _____
   _____
3. _____
   _____

4. _____
   _____

5. _____
   _____

Write down at least five *positive* messages that your subconscious mind has sent you in your lifetime. Think of situations where you did something and then afterward wondered why you did it and couldn't think of a conscious reason for it. Or maybe a thought or a good idea popped into your head and you did know where it came from.

1. _____
   _____

2. _____
   _____

3. _____
   _____

4. _____
   _____

5. _____
   _____

You want to focus on replacing the negative messages from your subconscious mind with positive messages. This is a process that you can do for the rest of your life. If you have a great day you can still do these to make it even better or ensure that tomorrow will be even better.

> **PLEASE, STOP AND COMPLETE THIS WRITTEN EXERCISE BEFORE GOING ON!**
>
> **BE PART OF THE SUCCESSFUL 2 PERCENT AND COMPLETE THE EXERCISE NOW!**

I use three methods to communicate with my subconscious:

First, I take naps to transfer information into my subconscious. I learned this from Thomas Edison, the great inventor. He would take short "power naps" during the day that he claimed were equal to a full nights sleep.

When I was studying to become an accountant, I often got tired and felt that my brain was full and couldn't absorb one more piece of information. So I would put my head down on the desk and take a fifteen-minute nap. When I woke up, it was like just waking up first thing in the morning. I felt completely rested, and my conscious mind felt completely empty so I could continue to study and absorb more information. I truly believe that this gave me a great advantage over some other students. They would get tired of studying but instead of napping and continuing, they would stop for the day. Effectively I could do twice as much studying in a day because of the naps.

The second method I use to communicate with my subconscious mind is meditation. I believe that meditation is a very important part of using our minds to their full potential. Meditation is nothing more than concentrating on a certain subject for an extended period of time. Many people tend to think for a very brief period of time and then take some form of action. But meditation requires thinking about the issue at hand for a longer time. Done correctly, it involves both the conscious and subconscious minds working in harmony. The result is usually a far better understanding of the subject on which you are meditating.

The third method I use is to listen to my subconscious mind. I believe strongly that what you put into your mind consciously, especially late at night, is what your subconscious mind works with while we're asleep. Your dreams are nothing but your subconscious mind working out how ideas fit together. Therefore, to use this to your advantage, you can think about a problem that you're trying to solve. Just before going to sleep at night, you can review the problem and all the information related to it. Then you can "ask" your subconscious mind to work on it. Usually, after doing this for a few days, you will wake up with the answer to the problem. Often you wouldn't have thought of this solution by working it out consciously.

SPIRIT

You communicate with your Spirit through prayer and meditation. Prayer isn't just something you do at church, and it doesn't have to be long and involved or spoken in Latin or King James English. Prayer is any communication that you have directly with the Spirit that resides inside you. Some common names for it are the Spirit, the Holy Ghost, the Holy Spirit, the Divine Spark, the true self, the inner self, the Higher Power, the Source, and the Center. Whatever you call it, recognize that it exists and is important to your success in life. Spirit is where you develop faith and beliefs and values. Spirit is what gives you your sense of what is right and wrong.

How does Spirit affect you in everyday life? Let's say you're studying for the CPA exams. If you believe you can pass, then you can pass. But if you believe you'll fail, then you'll fail. Amazingly, what you believe about yourself will come true.

Even though negative thoughts may have been planted in your subconscious mind by your parents when you were a child, you don't have to continue to listen to those thoughts. Your Spirit comes from God, and it tells you the truth if you will take the time to listen to it.

When I was preparing for my CPA exams, my family and friends were telling me that passing was impossible, that I couldn't do it because the CPA exams were very difficult. Based on my track record in academics, I should have listened to them and done something else. But I didn't because my Spirit was telling me that I could do anything I chose to do and that I was worthy of such a success. If my Spirit hadn't told me all these positive messages, my life would be much different today.

Prayer is talking to your Spirit,
and meditation is listening to it

Prayer is talking to your Spirit, and meditation is listening to it. When you pray, you talk to your Spirit, telling it what's going on, and asking it questions. When you meditate, or concentrate on something for an extended period, you communicate with your subconscious mind and your Spirit. You listen to what they have to say. I believe that your Spirit is stronger than your subconscious. If the two are at odds with each other, problems will result. For example, my Spirit overrode my subconscious when I was studying for my CPA exams. But long term, this difference couldn't work. I had to work hard to bring the two into alignment.

An excellent example of what this conflict between the subconscious mind and the Spirit can do was illustrated in the movie *Shine* starring Geoffrey Rush. This is the true story of David Holfgott, a world famous classical pianist. The main character, David, was born to a father who had been in the

Nazi concentration camps during World War II. In that environment, a person didn't want to get noticed for anything, good or bad, because it could easily lead to death.

However, the son was gifted to be a great pianist and found his gift early in life. He went against his father's wishes and went off to become a famous pianist in London. However, while his Spirit was leading him to be an inspired pianist, his subconscious mind still held the negative programming that his father had given him. Eventually he was unable to perform on stage. The two were in such strong opposition that he had a mental and emotional breakdown and couldn't play for years.

Inspiration is such an important part of your life, but you often don't think about where it comes from or how to find it. You won't find it in your body or in your mind, but you will find it in your Spirit. If you think about some of the great accomplishments in history, you see that people were inspired to do things that seemed impossible at the time.

Michelangelo, who painted the ceiling of the Sistine Chapel in Rome, was a man who was truly inspired. He worked for years under strenuous circumstances at a job that seemed impossible. Today people come from all over the world to see his work. Upon seeing the Sistine Chapel it is clear that he was truly inspired. That inspiration came from the Spirit inside of him.

SUMMARY

Communication with the body, the mind, and the Spirit is vital to your success in life. If you use only one or two parts of this triad, you won't reach your full potential. But if you harness all three, you'll reach a level of success that you could not have imagined earlier in your life.

This chapter talked about the relationship among the three facets of your being. The next three chapters will discuss each facet individually and how each one works in your life. I feel that this is the foundation of a successful life. *While goals give you the direction in your life, these three facets of your being are the foundation that you must understand and utilize because they give you the power to achieve your goals.*

A wonderful book on this subject is *Think and Grow Rich* by Napoleon Hill. It's not a book about making lots of money but about how to achieve success. It's an easy book to read and still very powerful after all these years. It is all about communication among the body, mind, and Spirit and how to maximize your potential.

Chapter Six

BODY = HEALTH & ENERGY

*The journey of a thousand miles
Begins with a single step*
—**Lao Tzu**

In the world of today, many people are allowing their bodies to suffer from neglect and abuse. Neglect is the passive acceptance of the world around us. They don't do the things that they should to stay healthy. The two keys to health (what a person eats and how a person exercises) are ignored.

Abuse is the active doing of things that harm an individual's body. Excess of any kind is bad for a human body. Too much food, alcohol, drugs, cigarettes, sugar, etc. cause a slow deterioration. Unfortunately, the damage isn't apparent until much later in life when it may be too late to repair.

Good health should be the first priority of everyone.

GOOD HEALTH IS FREEDOM AND ENERGY

The idea that good health gives you freedom and energy seems like such a simple one. However, many in North America don't seem to realize it. Did people who became obese have obesity as their goal in life? How about drug addicts or alcoholics? Was acquiring that addiction their goal in life? If you don't define what success is in the area of health, you can easily get into trouble. In today's world there are excesses of so many of the bad things in life. Food, drugs, alcohol, etc. are plentiful and cheap. In addition, people are constantly bombarded with messages that tempt a person to get involved in unhealthy habits. Just think of these messages are common in every day life:

- Beer commercials picture healthy, beautiful young people having lots of fun. They don't show the alcoholic living on the street because he can't hold down a job.
- Commercials and movies depict cigarettes as sexy, but there's nothing sexy about kissing a smoker or dying of lung cancer.
- Food for kids is usually advertised as tasting good and being fun. Food for dogs and cats is usually shown as being healthy and nutritious. As a result, we have a country full of healthy pets with shiny fur coats and a lot of children with weight and health problems.

- Commercials can persuade people with medical problems that the solution is easy: they can just take a pill. This results in bad health habits and addictions to prescription drugs.
- Car commercials show that a new car will make you happy and attract friends and maybe a lover. But years of payments on a depreciating vehicle add stress to life and often relationships. Car payments can start a person down the road to excessive personal debt.

Selling unhealthy products can be very profitable, so lots of companies promote these products.

When you're encouraged to purchase a food product, the promoter may not have your best interest at heart. There isn't much advertisement about eating properly because there's less profit in it. Food companies make more profit if you buy more food. Many foods in America contain sugar or high fructose corn syrup (even worse than sugar), which the majority of Americans are addicted to (yes, addicted!). Diet companies succeed if you fail. Just think, are they truly interested in your success? Alcohol and cigarette companies do much better when you do worse.

You don't see many advertisements for eating whole grains, eating healthy, or becoming a vegetarian or vegan. Attitudes are so skewed that people who are overweight are considered normal and people with healthy habits are considered *health nuts*. If you want to be healthy, you must figure out how to do so for yourself and avoid societal peer pressure and potential ostracization by many people. The resources are there for you to learn if you make the effort.

Also, when you travel or eat out in restaurants, it can be difficult to find healthy food choices. I know that I have become hesitant about eating out as much as I did because I find restaurant food is not usually what I like to eat. First, it is usually much more salty than I would eat at home. I do not own a salt shaker. Secondly, the selection of healthy food is often smaller and less desirable that I like. Often the healthy dishes are just modified versions of the unhealthy dishes. Thirdly, the portion sizes are usually larger than necessary. Many of us grew up with aren't that taught us to clean our plates which is not a good habit.

But it can be done. Being healthy is certainly possible. It's very easy in this age of information to find out how to live a healthy life by simply adopting a few good habits and sticking to them. When eating out it takes stronger self-discipline but it certainly can be done.

Also, it doesn't mean going on a diet and doing without for the rest of your life. It means eating what you want, but doing so in a way that keeps you healthy and well. The belief that healthy foods taste bad and unhealthy foods taste good is a myth. Once you eat healthy foods regularly you will find that they taste wonderful. However, it takes a period of time to lose the cravings for the unhealthy food.

Maintaining a healthy weight is simple. Calories in must not exceed calories out. In other words, what you eat each day must only be equivalent to what you use up that day. Unfortunately, while the concept may be simple, putting it into practice may not be easy.

Good health gives you freedom. For example, proper weight and regular exercise make it easier to walk, get in and out of cars or planes, play with your children or grandchildren, participate in many hobbies, and many other activities. This is especially true as people age. Also, they mean fewer health problems and less time spent at doctors' offices. It is amazing how eating properly will make you feel better as well as maintain a healthy weight. It is actually easy to maintain good health if you set that as a priority every day.

Even though many Americans are very concerned about health care, they don't seem to care about their health. *If you spend a little effort on good health and therefore the prevention of bad health, you will need health care less.* Taking care of your health is being proactive and can be done to prevent bad health. Going to the doctor with bad health is reactive and is done after the damage is done.

PERSONAL GROWTH EXERCISE:

This exercise helps you become aware of your weaknesses or addictions. Take a few minutes and write down what you might be addicted to. If you say you're not addicted to anything, ask yourself these questions:

Could I go one month without eating sugar? Explain.

_____
_____
_____

Could I go one month without drinking alcohol? Explain.

_____
_____
_____

Could I go one month without smoking? Explain.

_____
_____
_____

Could I go one month without taking drugs? Explain.

_____
_____
_____

Could I go one month without television? Explain.

_____
_____
_____

Could I go one month without coffee? Explain.

_____
_____
_____

Is there something else in your life that you do that you feel it would be difficult giving up? Explain.

_____
_____
_____

Now, describe how much this addiction affects your life.

Does it cause you health issues?

_____
_____
_____

Does it affect your studies or your job?

_____
_____
_____

Does it affect your relationships?

_____
_____
_____

Does it affect your attitude?

_____
_____
_____

> **PLEASE, STOP AND COMPLETE THIS WRITTEN EXERCISE BEFORE GOING ON!**
>
> **BE PART OF THE SUCCESSFUL 2 PERCENT AND COMPLETE THE EXERCISE NOW!**

Many books have been written about health, eating, and exercise. My best advice to you is to keep it simple and always keep having a healthy body as your goal. A healthy body will mean more energy and fewer health problems. People often say they don't have time to exercise and eat right. Well, they seem to find the time for sick days and doctor visits when their health fails. For example Brian, a salesman, never took time for good health. But he was constantly sick, missing work and unable to do other things because of bad health. He made many visits to the doctor each year. The lesson here is that by spending a little time now on health, you will enjoy your life more and save lots of time and cost later on.

What does a healthy life require? There are two important aspects to maintaining good health: (1) eating and (2) exercising. You can maintain good health by following good eating habits and getting regular exercise.

EAT TO BE HEALTHY

> *There is no magic bullet.*
> *You have to eat healthy and*
> *Live healthy to be healthy*
> *And look healthy.*
> *End of story.*
> **—Morgan Spurlock**

The following list contains good eating behaviors to follow:

- Eat whole grains for breakfast
- Eat mostly vegetables during the day, preferably raw or steamed
- Eat fruit for snacks
- Eat four to six small meals or snacks daily
- Drink lots of water
- Finish eating and drinking liquids before seven o'clock in the evening (three to four hours before bedtime)
- Avoid fad diets

- Seek good nutrition not pleasure with food
- Don't punish yourself for overeating or eating the wrong things; just try to do better tomorrow
- Read books about health and nutrition
- Consider the benefits of fasting (with the help of a medical professional)
- Use the 80/20 rule (explained in the following paragraph)

Let's begin with the Pareto Principle or the 80/20 rule, which applies to many situations. The rule states that 80 percent of a business's profits come from 20 percent of its activity. In addition, 80 percent of its problems come from 20 percent of its customers. If we think about our own lives, there are many areas where this might apply. For example, I spent 80 percent of my time as a professor with 20 percent of my students, who were having problems.

How can you apply this rule to eating and exercising to be healthy? One of the reasons that people fail or don't even try to be healthier is that they feel that they must be perfect all the time. Not true! You need to do the things that will make you healthy most of the time (80 percent), but you have the leeway to not follow these habits part of the time (20 percent). If you do the right thing 80 percent of the time (five or six days a week) and fall off for 20 percent of the time (one or two days a week), you will end up healthier. What

BODY = HEALTH & ENERGY

you may discover is that being healthy is enjoyable, so you may not to want to stray from the path.

When I started to become more concerned about my health, I talked to my daughter, who is my health guru, and she told me about whole grains. I had always enjoyed vegetables and fruits; they were the mainstay of my eating. However, in the morning, I always ate boxed cereals. It was scary to read the labels because they indicated that the cereals had many bad things in them, especially sugar in its various forms. Once I switched to preparing whole grains for breakfast, my weight dropped. I felt much better because I had stopped taking all those bad chemicals and sugar into my body and instead was eating very healthy food with lots of nutrients and fiber. Whole grains are inexpensive, easy to prepare and can be purchased at many health food stores. I now have the philosophy that I don't want to eat processed foods such as those that come in a box or a can.

When I was in my twenties I noticed a pattern when I ate breakfast that contained sugar. Eating cereal with sugar or toast with jam or jelly for breakfast would cause an energy surge called a *sugar high*. However, later in the morning, when the sugar high was gone, I would crave more sugar to replace it. This created an energy roller coaster of sugar highs followed by crashes and strong cravings. This is a common problem when eating foods with sugar. Over time this can lead to diabetes.

Another problem is that many people in our country seem obsessed with dieting and losing weight. Diets (temporary changes in eating habits) are often an unbalanced, unnatural way of eating and don't work in the long term. So, never diet!

PERSONAL GROWTH EXERCISE:

Before you go on, take a few minutes to write responses to these prompts about eating habits.

1. Describe how you feel about your current weight. Men tend to be optimistic and women tend to be pessimistic when it comes to their weight.

_____
_____
_____

2. List five things that you can do today to improve your eating habits to be healthier. Don't write "go on a diet". Instead, list ways to amend your eating habits a little bit at a time. Review this list often.

_____
_____
_____
_____

BODY = HEALTH & ENERGY

3. Check your Body Mass Index (BMI). This can be found on the internet. What does your BMI indicate?

_____
_____
_____

4. If you're having a problem with your eating habits, try the 30 Day Challenge at the end of chapter 4 to make a change in the next thirty days.

_____
_____
_____

> **PLEASE, STOP AND COMPLETE THIS WRITTEN EXERCISE BEFORE GOING ON!**
>
> **BE PART OF THE SUCCESSFUL 2 PERCENT AND COMPLETE THE EXERCISE NOW!**

EXERCISE TO BE HEALTHY

*When it comes to health,
Diet is the Queen, but
Exercise is the King*
—**Jack LaLanne**

The following list contains good exercise behaviors to follow:

- Exercise to maintain flexibility, muscle tone, and a strong heart
- Perform basic exercises for fifteen to thirty minutes, three to five times a week
- Perform aerobic exercises for at least thirty minutes, three to five times a week
- Don't try to lose weight through exercise alone. Weight loss is best accomplished by combining exercise with a change in eating habits
- Learn how to breathe properly using your diaphragm
- Read books on physical fitness
- Walk for at least one hour a day

I could spend a thousand pages talking about exercise, but I just want to describe a simple plan that you can follow at home with a small outlay of cash. You don't need gym memberships and fancy workout clothes to be healthy. All you need is to make exercise a priority in your life. However, if a health club makes that easier for you, then by all means go for it.

Personally, I've never liked structured exercise programs. I have kept in shape all my life simply by being physically active. I hike, ride my bike, and walk every chance I get. This always seemed to be enough. All my life I tried to eat healthy foods but never followed a particular plan. This worked for me most of my life, but I noticed that as I age, two things happened. First, I gained a little weight and second, I seemed less flexible and my muscles less toned.

Concerning the issue of flexibility and muscle tone, I thought of my former boss in California. I went to visit him when he was in his seventies, and he told me that he went to the gym to work out daily. I was surprised because I wondered why a man in his seventies would want to have really big muscles. He said that he wasn't trying to build muscle; he was just trying to keep what he already had. Flexibility is a real issue as you age, so there is a real advantage to exercising.

I like to spend time exercising because I find the rhythm of repetitions is very peaceful and relaxing. In addition afterward I feel extremely energized. I decided to design a simple exercise plan that I could do at home. Home is more comfortable than a gym, and exercising at home saves time.

You should keep exercise simple. In his book, *Body for Life*, Bill Phillips gives examples of exercise programs. Bill Phillips is a bodybuilder but I don't go for the bodybuilding part of his book. However, the advice is very good for improving fitness. I do some of the exercises he recommends three to five days a week. It has done wonders for my flexibility and muscle tone.

Each day I vary which exercises I do and how many I do. The total cost of my exercise program was less than a hundred dollars, which included the book and a simple set of free weights. Remember to start off slowly and build up gradually. Unless you're planning to enter a bodybuilding contest, you have no reason to get buff. All you want is to get toned as part of being healthy.

Want to know something amazing? All my life I hated running, but a few years ago I had an uncontrollable urge to run. Now I love running. I run three times a week for between fifteen and twenty miles each week. I have run a half marathon, and eventually I want to run a full marathon. My running is truly unbelievable to me. I never thought that I could run these distances and really enjoy them.

PERSONAL GROWTH EXERCISE:

Before you go on, take a few minutes to review your exercise activity.

1. Describe how you feel about your flexibility, muscle tone, and heart health.

_____
_____
_____

2. How often do you exercise?

_____
_____
_____

3. List five things you can do starting today to exercise better.

_____
_____
_____
_____
_____

4. If you're having a problem getting started with an exercise program, try the 30 Day Challenge at the end of chapter 4 to make a change in the next thirty days.

_____
_____
_____

Warning: exercise can cause weight gain. Here is a trap that people sometimes fall into after exercising: you feel that you just had a great workout and burned off a lot of calories, so you believe that you can now go to the coffee shop and have a latte and a sweet. The bad news is that the snack you consume probably contains more calories than what you just burned off. I gained weight when I started running, and it definitely was not all muscle. As you lose fat and gain muscle, weight lose may seem slow – but muscle mass is desirable weight.

> **PLEASE, STOP AND COMPLETE THIS WRITTEN EXERCISE BEFORE GOING ON!**
>
> **BE PART OF THE SUCCESSFUL 2 PERCENT AND COMPLETE THE EXERCISE NOW!**

SUMMARY

Sensible eating and exercise work hand in hand to a healthy body. If you eat more vegetables, fruits and whole grains and fewer processed foods, you can maintain the right weight and be healthier. Exercise that is regular is very beneficial.

The greatest benefit of exercise may not be physical but the wonderful change in attitude.

Chapter Seven

MIND = KNOWLEDGE, DISCIPLINE & WISDOM

Your mind is a garden
Your thoughts are your seeds;
You can grow flowers or
You can grow weeds.
—Anonymous

Did you know that your mind is one of the most powerful instruments on earth? The human mind is capable of so much more than anyone can imagine. I believe that great people in history like Thomas Edison and Benjamin Franklin were so successful because they learned how to use their minds better than others.

You can learn to use your mind more if you just learn to feed and exercise it. That's correct, just like a healthy body, a healthy mind needs to be fed good material regularly and exercised on a daily basis.

You should never reach the point in life where you stop learning.

When I use the word "mind", I am referring to more than a person's brain. I consider the thinking process, will, and emotions as part of the mind. I will look at them as one since they operate together.

KNOWLEDGE

I believe that a person's mind is the single greatest under-utilized asset. You could accomplish so much more if you utilized a greater portion of your mind's potential. I believe that a lot of the great people in history did amazing things because they found a way to use a larger percentage of their mind's power.

There is an old saying that an idle mind is the devil's playground or devil's workshop. This relates to the unused portion of your mind. Since you are not using your mind to its capacity, there is a lot of extra activity going on that doesn't necessarily work for your benefit. It has always amazed me that humans seem designed with evil as the default setting. If children are left alone for a while, what happens? They often get into trouble. If teenagers are left alone without anything to do, what happens? They often get into trouble. This even applies to adults. If adults don't have enough to do, they often end up getting into trouble. It seems to me that people have to work at being good and leading a good life.

On the other hand, if a person uses their mind more fully, it is amazing what can be accomplished. I know I've done things that have amazed me. In high school I felt that I couldn't accomplish much or learn hard subjects like calculus and physics. To my surprise, I ended up becoming an accountant in Canada and later in California. I took the exams in both countries and passed them the first time. I earned a bachelor's degree and a master's degree and went on to be a professor for twenty-five years. In retirement I became an author and write books. I feel that I figured out how to use more of my mind's potential. *I believe that you can do amazing things if you want and if you are willing to apply yourself.*

I truly believe that I can do almost anything I put my mind to it and apply myself. When I started in junior high school, I had a terrible attitude problem. In high school I had an even worse attitude problem. I just was not a happy camper and I did not want to be there. This was all related to my childhood home being a place that would make a person crazy. My attitude didn't improve when I got to university, but I still managed to pass all of my courses, even if just barely. After I graduated from university, I felt lost and didn't know what I wanted to do. I was bored and wanted some direction in life, so I took some night classes at a local university.

When I took accounting, I felt like I had just hit a home run: I found what I was destined to do. I had always enjoyed math and was good at it, so accounting was a great fit. But even more than that was how accounting was set up. In grade eight I had a business mowing lawns. I established a set of books to keep track of my income and expenses. I put the expenses on the left and the income on the right. The difference between the two columns was my profit. I had designed this as a teenager all by myself. I was amazed to learn that that's exactly how accounting systems are set up in business. I felt completely at home with this subject.

In my twenties, I quit my job as an officer in the Canadian Navy and took a position as an accountant in training. This required a fifty percent pay cut. This was a job that I really loved. Since I never thought that I was smart, I worked hard. I realized that I didn't really know the proper techniques of studying, so I approached some really successful students and asked them how they studied. They told me their techniques, and I used them. In accounting classes, I was usually in the top five on exams, and I was one of the top students overall in our finals. I averaged 90 percent on my CPA exams, which the majority of students don't even pass.

I had the ability, talent, skill, aptitude, whatever you want to call it inside me all along. It was only when I started studying accounting that I tapped into it. What if I had never taken that night class and discovered my ability to do accounting? It is important to know that you already have everything inside you that you need to live a fulfilling life. You just have to *discover* it and then *develop* it.

Now, you may be saying that I was lucky to find my talent. You're right that I was extremely lucky because it has made all the difference in my life. But I didn't just stumble upon it one day while I was walking aimlessly through life. I was in a job that I really disliked and wanted to leave, so I had to ask, for what other job? I took classes at university for a few years without success until I found the accounting class. I discovered it because I was searching for it.

Later, I had the knowledge and the desire to teach, but I was completely incapable of speaking in front of a group of people. You may feel uncomfortable with public speaking, but I was absolutely terrified. An opportunity came up with a group called Toastmasters. The club teaches people how to speak in public. They are located all over the world.

Within eight weeks I was leading the meeting and enjoying every minute of it. Once again, this wasn't some great feat that I accomplished. It was something inside of me that I *discovered* and *developed*. This led me to be what God had designed me to be, a teacher.

I strongly recommend Toastmasters to you. The teach public speaking which you may feel that you don't need. However, there are two amazing benefits to learning to speak to a group of people. One is that you will become a better leader. But I feel that the greatest benefit is that you will develop a greater self-confidence that will spill over into all areas of your life.

MENTAL FOOD AND EXERCISE

> *Once you learn to read,*
> *You will be forever free.*
> **—Frederick Douglass**

Just like your body needs to be fed and exercised, your mind needs to be fed and exercised also. Many people do this only when forced to. Often people stop learning after they leave school. If you do that, you will severely limit your level of success in all areas of your life. Instead, you should be learning new things all the time. You should be learning about work, personal growth, hobbies, relationships and everything else. You have to guard against being passive and watching too much television. When you watch television, you are seeing someone else live life while you're not living yours. I understand that you might like something on television, but it just doesn't make sense to spend so much time watching others. I get a kick out of the reality shows. Some people go on an adventure, and you get to watch. *It would be better if you got up and went out on your own adventure!*

(PS Reality shows aren't real)

What does your mind like to eat? Lots! Your mind is hungry and wants to be fed. If you don't feed it good stuff, it will be eating junk food. You could listen to a motivational speaker or read books that will teach you new things. If you are watching television, your mind is digesting commercials and the lessons in the television shows. You will not lead a happy, successful life if you fill your mind with these ideas. Remember *garbage in, garbage out*.

People always argue that there are some good shows on television. I could argue that there is some good stuff in the garbage truck. But I don't want it dumped in my yard so I can pick out the good stuff, because I'll also be stuck with all the bad stuff. Do you feel that the time you spend watching television is spent wisely? You need to consider how your life could be changed if you reduced the time you spend watching television.

The national average is that a person watches four to six hours of television a day. That is one-third of the time that we're awake each day. What do you gain from this huge time investment? Is your life any richer? What else could you be doing with that time? You could earn a university degree. You could be involved in your favorite hobbies. You could volunteer at your church or in a community activity.

Just think that if you reduced your television time by two hours a day, it would add up to be 730 hours a year or 91 eight hour work days or 4 work months. What could you accomplish if you spent an additional 4 months a year in some type of productive activity?

The garbage in, garbage out idea also applies to reading. There are a lot of good books from which you can learn something and that will inspire you in some way. Choose books that will motivate you.

I recommend that you decide to learn something new and then make it a goal and focus on achieving that goal. One time in my life when I felt particularly lost, I set the goal of getting my MBA. That goal spurred my mind, and not only did I get an MBA, but I also got my CPA license and a new life in California. For years I've read self-help books, listened to motivational speakers, and read my Bible regularly. I have also avoided watching television most of my life. Would you believe that I do not even own a television set? All of this feeding of my mind has been wonderful—it's made my life much richer.

Next let's look at exercising your mind. *Like your body, your mind needs to be fed and exercised.* How do you exercise your mind? Use it! How you accomplish that depends on your stage of life and what else is going on in your life. You can take a degree or just take a course that interests you. You can find a hobby that interests you. You can learn just for fun. Speaking another language is a valuable skill to learn. Most people in the world speak more than one language. What about playing a musical instrument? The opportunities are endless.

> *Like your body, your mind needs to be fed and exercised*

You can join a book club or Bible study that requires you to read, think, and then talk about what you read. Reading in this way is more challenging than just reading a novel. Some people do crossword puzzles or Sudoku to keep their minds sharp.

Do you lack the self-discipline to set up a program of study and then follow it? There are many preset programs that you can take join. You could check out a community college, community center, recreation department, or the internet. If you commit yourself to learning and doing your absolute best, you may change your life in ways you never dreamed possible.

Remember the theory of Earl Nightingale that if you do something for one hour a day, in three years you will be an expert at it. Just think what would happen if you gave up just two hours of television a day and devoted those two hours to something you wanted to accomplish. You could learn how to play a musical instrument, speak a new language, or do anything you desire.

You might think this doesn't sound like a great deal of fun. You can still do the things that you like; all I'm suggesting is that you spend some time on improving your health and your mind. The rewards will far outweigh the costs in the long run. Besides, learning something that you want to learn is fun!

PERSONAL GROWTH EXERCISE:

List 5 television shows that you currently watch on a regular basis:

1. _____
2. _____
3. _____
4. _____
5. _____

MIND = KNOWLEDGE, DISCIPLINE & WISDOM

Do you feel that watching these shows adds value to your life? Describe below:

_____
_____
_____

List 5 things you can do instead of watching television:

1. _____
2. _____
3. _____
4. _____
5. _____

Describe how these 5 things would improve the quality of your life:

_____
_____
_____

PLEASE, STOP AND COMPLETE THIS WRITTEN EXERCISE BEFORE GOING ON!

BE PART OF THE SUCCESSFUL 2 PERCENT AND COMPLETE THE EXERCISE NOW!

DISCIPLINE

> *Seek freedom and*
> *Become captive of your desires.*
> *Seek discipline and*
> *Find your liberty.*
> **—Frank Herber**

Your mind has awesome potential. When you get to later chapters, you'll see that a great deal of your potential is centered in your mind. One of the greatest ways your mind can unleash your potential is to provide discipline. *Self-discipline is simply doing what you should do even when it's not what you want to do.* I know that many people in society today don't like external discipline. Internal discipline, or self-discipline, is even more difficult. To discipline yourself is hard because you typically rebel against external discipline, so when you attempt self-discipline, you would be rebelling against yourself. That is why many people fall down when it comes to self-discipline.

Self-discipline is simply doing what you should; even when it's not what you want to do

Have you heard of the "Law of Liberty"? I know that sounds like a paradox because the word *law* usually means a restriction of freedom. *The Law of Liberty refers to self-discipline, or restricting what you do in one part of life so that you have more freedom in another part.*

For example, you have the freedom to use drugs. If you don't do drugs, you give up that freedom. If you exercise your freedom to use drugs, you may become a slave to drugs. However, if you use self-discipline and don't use drugs, you will be free from the consequences of drug use and experience freedom. Do you know anyone who has used drugs for a long time and who has freedom in his or her life? The same is true with food, alcohol, sex, pornography, television, the internet, and anything else when used to excess. If you don't exercise self-discipline, these habits can take over your life. There's often a fine line between enjoying something and being addicted to it.

Another important area of your life is financial freedom. You have the freedom to borrow and buy far more than is reasonable. If you exercise self-discipline in financial matters, you will be free to do what you can afford. If you don't exercise self-discipline in this area, you end up with excessive debt and the inability to repay it. That is a huge loss of freedom and is often emotionally devastating. If you have any kind of debt other than a mortgage then you should look at your financial situation. Also, if you don't have savings then you should look at your financial situation. A wonderful source of help is the Financial Peace University with Dave Ramsey.

How do you develop self-discipline? I believe that it comes from a strong desire to accomplish something. If you set a goal, either formally or informally, and you have a strong desire to achieve that goal, you will have self-discipline. Self-discipline is used in two ways. First, you do the things that you want to do. Secondly, you don't do the things that you don't want to do. I see so many people who don't do the things that are good for them but continue to do the things that are bad for them.

Look at professional athletes: some of them exhibit poor self-discipline off the field, getting into all kinds of trouble. But on the field, they exhibit good self-discipline because they really want to be successful at their sport. It really stands out if an athlete shows poor self-discipline on the playing field.

I believe that you can develop self-discipline just like any other habit. To improve your self-discipline, you read motivational books. The books deal with how to use your mind to improve your life. They help you know how to think, how to set goals, how to motivate yourself, how to follow a plan, and how to modify the plan or a behavior if it needs to change.

The mind is much more powerful than most people realize. *What you believe has great power.* For example, I have always believed that I won't get sick. By sick I mean colds, flu and seasonal illnesses. I have this as a firm belief, and it has held true for my whole life. In the past thirty years, I have not missed a single day of work or play due to illness. When I was teaching, I typically had about 150 students in my classes from all over the world who were often sick with colds, the flu, and heaven only knows what else. Yet in twenty-five years of teaching, I never missed a day due to illness. Why? I simply don't believe in it.

I have a friend who believes that she will get a cold each winter. She further believes that the cold will take ten days to come on, be around for an additional ten days, and take ten days more to leave, for a total of thirty days with the cold. When she first feels sick, she has it in her mind that the cold is going to last thirty days. Guess what—it lasts thirty days. What you put into your mind and what you believe will be what you experience in life.

I recently read a book called *The Biology of Belief* by Bruce H. Lipton that validates this belief. People have often scoffed at me when I tell them I don't believe in getting sick. But this book states that the medical community is coming to realize that the very cells in your body will respond to what you believe and change and make it come true. Because I believed I wouldn't get sick, my body responded in such a way as to prevent me from getting sick. Conversely, my friend's body responded by letting her get sick for thirty days each winter.

I believe that when a medicine works, its effects are partly due to our minds and partly due to the chemicals themselves. You've heard stories about studies in which patients were given a placebo and did every bit as well as people who took medicines. Why do flu shots work? I think that often they work because people who get them *believe* that they're protected. Why don't some flu shots work? I think some people still get the flu even after the flu shot because their belief that they'll get the flu is stronger than their belief that the flu shot will work.

You can program your mind so that you can do whatever you want to do. Can you be healthy? Yes. Can you give up a bad habit? Yes. Can you have the career of your dreams? Yes. Can you find the soul mate that you have always longed for? Yes. I firmly believe that you can do almost anything you want with your mind.

PERSONAL GROWTH EXERCISE:

Describe how you feed your mind:

Do you read books that help you learn more about your career or hobbies?

_____

_____

_____

MIND = KNOWLEDGE, DISCIPLINE & WISDOM

Do you attend seminars where you learn a new skill?

_____
_____
_____

Do you pollute your mind with gossip (e.g., from tabloids)?

_____
_____
_____

Do you pollute your mind with television?

_____
_____
_____

Do you pollute your mind with bad news?

_____
_____
_____

PLEASE, STOP AND COMPLETE THIS WRITTEN EXERCISE BEFORE GOING ON!

BE PART OF THE SUCCESSFUL 2 PERCENT AND COMPLETE THE EXERCISE NOW!

YOU BECOME WHAT YOU THINK

Whatever the mind can conceive and believe,
It can achieve.
—Napoleon Hill

One of the great beliefs of scholars, philosophers, and prophets throughout history has been that *you become what you think about.* This is both powerful and scary. It states that you have control over your own life. You are the only one who controls your thoughts (unless you give that power away to someone else), and your thoughts are what you become.

You become what you think
about most of the time

The mind is to your life as a pilot is to an airplane. The pilot is the center of control and directs the plane. The pilot can make it go up or down, east or west, and take off and land safely. Plane crashes often happen because the pilot wasn't doing what was supposed to be done.

Your mind works the same way in your life. If you fill your mind with good material, then it has good thoughts and attitudes, and you experience good outcomes in your life. However, if you fill your mind with bad material, then you have bad thoughts and attitudes, and you experience bad outcomes in life. It is not what happens to you in life but how you perceive and respond to what happens to you that will determine how happy you are.

Your mind is a powerful tool. Many people use only a small fraction of the brains' capacity. Are you one of those people who believe that you don't have to learn anymore? Do you associate learning with study and you don't want to study? The mind is a tool that you can use to change your life. So why not do it!

Just think about it: you have the power to determine your level of happiness. That is an awesome power and a huge responsibility. Using it properly doesn't come naturally for most people. You must learn how to do it wisely.

You enter the world as babies screaming and demanding what you want when you want it. You reach maturity when you learn to balance your own life and not scream and demand. Maturity means that you decide what it is that you want in life and then seek it in a rational manner.

WISDOM

*By three methods we may learn wisdom:
First, by reflection, which is noblest;
Second, by imitation, which is easiest; and
Third by experience, which is the bitterest."*
—Confucius

You may think that wisdom comes with age because you must first gather information and then organize it into knowledge. Then, you must have life experiences, both positive and negative, to help you learn how to use the knowledge you possess. Once you can apply knowledge to your life you have wisdom. Wisdom doesn't come automatically as you age. It also depends on your ability to learn and apply what you have learned.

My definition of *wisdom is the application of knowledge to a given situation.* I also believe that the ability to apply knowledge comes from your life experiences. Wisdom seems to come with age simply because you gain more knowledge and experience the older you get. However, some younger individuals are wise while some older individuals are not. Wisdom doesn't come automatically as we age. It also depends on your ability to learn and apply what you have learned.

I believe that gaining wisdom is an admirable goal. Getting an education and gaining knowledge are great, but if you can't apply what you have learned, what's the purpose? Some entrepreneurs don't have a great education, but they're successful because they learned what they needed to know and were very good at applying it to their business. For example, I studied what made some business people successful. One of the most important determining factors was their ability to pick the right person for a job. This ability comes from wisdom.

Everyone has wisdom to some degree. Wisdom can be broken down into many categories, two of which are worldly wisdom and Godly wisdom. The more worldly wisdom you possess, the more financially successful you will be. However, the more Godly wisdom you possess, the more peace, joy, and contentment you will experience. A balance between the two is best.

SUMMARY

Why don't you use more of your mind's capacity? It is baffling to me why people don't seem to want to use more of their brain capacity. It is free, has unlimited potential, and can make unbelievable changes in your life.

Everyone can use more of their mind. I really encourage you to look into what you would like to do with your mind. I'm sure the rewards will surprise you.

Just like your physical body, your mind needs to be fed and exercised or it will atrophy. If you make a conscious effort to feed your mind good material daily, it will improve your attitude immensely. If you exercise your mind not only will it be stronger but your life will expand with the new things undertaken.

Discipline sounds like a bad word to many people, but a little self-discipline can change your life dramatically and give you more freedom. The more you use self-discipline and see the benefits, the easier it'll be to use it in other situations as well.

Chapter Eight

SPIRIT = BELIEF, FAITH, CONFIDENCE & INSPIRATION

One life is all we have and
We live it as we believe in living it.
But to sacrifice what you are and
To live without belief,
That is a fate more terrible than dying.
—**Joan of Arc**

Many people don't like to talk about their spiritual beliefs. However, the fact is you all have a basis for your moral and ethical beliefs. This basis is founded on something within you.

It is critical that you examine and develop this foundation so that you can lead a successful life. No one has been successful in life without some code of ethical behavior as a guide.

Whatever your belief system may be, it is important to examine it and decide for yourself what you believe and don't believe about life and what your role is in it.

BELIEF

> *Be sure you put your feet in the right place,*
> *Then stand firm.*
> **—Abraham Lincoln**

Believing something and working toward it will make it come to be. I remember trying out for the football team in high school. I was asked to try out because of my size. However, I believed that I wouldn't make it because I wasn't competitive and didn't like football all that much. I probably didn't put my heart into the practices. At that time, I also had a job that I felt was important. I feel my desire to keep my job may have been stronger than my desire to play football. I remember talking one day with a friend who was also trying out. We weren't doing all that well. He was so gung-ho and fired up I couldn't believe it. I asked,

"How long do you plan to stick around?"

"Until I make it!" he answered quite simply.

I told him that if I was picked to play in the first game, I would stay. If not, then I planned to quit. Well, it's probably no surprise that I quit and went to work and that he stayed and eventually ended up playing. His beliefs led him to where he wanted to go and my beliefs led me to where I wanted to go.

The different parts of Spirit listed in the chapter title are overlapping. However, I feel that they each deserve a separate discussion. Belief is a powerful part of your success, and when you get to the *Rocks to Diamonds* part of the book, you'll see how important it is. *Belief underlies self-confidence and inspiration; it's a very important element for your success.*

Belief underlies self-confidence and inspiration

Let's look at how belief is a key element when you're learning a new skill like driving a car. When you learned to drive, the first time out, you were probably nervous and afraid to make a mistake. But after that first time out, when you had success and didn't hit anything, your belief in your ability to drive rose and so did your self-confidence. Each time you went out driving, your belief that you could do this rose and your self-confidence rose with it. Eventually you got to the point where your belief in your ability to drive switched to a *certainty*, and then you drove without really having to think about what you were doing.

What if you could raise your level of belief to certainty without repeated small successes to increase your self-confidence?

This would be a major leap forward. Well, that's what we will discuss in chapter 11. The better you can accomplish this, the faster you'll grow in whatever it is you're doing. Raising your belief to certainty is a key part of the *Rocks to Diamonds* program.

When I first started playing golf, I read an article about Jack Nicklaus, one of the greatest golfers of all time. One of his keys to success was visualization. Visualization is simply seeing in your mind exactly what you are going to do in a given situation.

People always wanted to know the secret to Jack Nicklaus' great success. One of his secrets was that he would play the entire course in his mind until he developed the certainty that he knew how to play it best. He would picture every shot in detail and see himself making the shot. Then he would picture the ball landing where he wanted it to. Before he even stepped onto the golf course for the first time, he was certain that he could play it well, and he usually did just that.

You can do that with almost anything. If you're starting to teach, you can picture yourself teaching a class with confidence and answering all your students' questions. When you enter the classroom, you'll be certain of success. When I'm going to perform in a play, I spend part of my rehearsal time picturing myself delivering my lines with ease and the audience's reaction. If I am going to give a speech, I picture past successes and then see myself giving my next speech successfully.

Do you believe visualization works? Often this technique is used backward, and unfortunately, it works both ways. Let's say that someone has to give a speech in front of a lot of people. (Public speaking is one of the most feared things that someone has to do in life. Public speaking often ranks above death when peoples' fears are studied.) What do most people do? They picture in their mind the speech that they're to give. But instead of picturing success, they picture failure. They see themselves forgetting everything that they wanted to say and standing there lost and tongue tied. What happens? They do exactly what they pictured, and they have now reinforced their belief that they can't speak in public. Their self-confidence decreases as a result. Their poor result reinforces the negative belief, so their performance gets worse as time goes on.

Visualization is a powerful tool that you can use for or against yourself. Why not use it to your advantage?

One belief that I assume you hold is a belief in God. If you don't believe in God, please keep an open mind and consider what I'm saying. Many successful people believe in God and base their lives upon that belief. I was very anti-church, but I always believed in God. At age thirty-five, I went back to church and started to learn more about God, and it made a huge difference in my life. If you don't believe in God, I believe you're missing the most important part of life.

When I was thirty-five, I hadn't been to church in over twenty years. When I started going again, I participated in a Bible study and met a man who explained it like this: if you believe in God and there is no God, you will have a better life here on earth and nothing will happen when you die. However, if you don't believe in God, and there is a God, then you'll have a worse life here on earth, and when you die, you'll live forever in hell. I'm not trying to threaten you but to just point out that belief in God and following God's teachings will make your life here on earth a whole lot better. The teachings in the Bible show how to live successful lives and how to be happy.

Think of God as the perfect parent who only wants you to be happy and successful. To that end, God's instructions on how to have a better life are written in the Bible. The closer you follow its rules, the better your life will be. Just think if the only laws in the country were the Ten Commandments (see End Note) and if everyone followed them. There would be no crime or conflict. People would get along well, and everyone would be happy. When you watch or read the news and see wars and criminal activity, most of the actions you see are violations of the Ten Commandments. If everyone followed these, it would immediately eliminate the need for the justice system.

God is like electricity. God is the energy in your life. Most people don't understand electricity even though they use it every day, all day. Even though they don't understand it and can't see it, they still believe in it and use it because it allows them to do what they want and have successful lives. If you were not plugged into electricity, you would have no power. But when you are plugged in, you have the power to do whatever you want.

To take advantage of electricity, you must take action to get connected. God powers your life through the Spirit inside you, like the wires in your house. *If you get connected to the Spirit within you, you will have unlimited power in your life.*

To connect an appliance to electricity, you use an electrical plug with three prongs. God also has three prongs, or parts: Father, Son, and Holy Spirit, each one distinct yet all part of one. The Spirit, which resides inside of you, is by far the most powerful of the three elements of your being: mind, body and Spirit. As I discussed in chapter 5, combining the three elements yields the greatest power. Remember I suggested that we assign weights to the three elements. If we give the body a weight of 10, then the mind would have a weight of 100, and the Spirit, being the most powerful, would have a weight of 1,000.

When we combine all three, we get:

Body x Mind X Spirit = Power
10 x 100 x 1,000 = 1,000,000

A person who uses all three parts in this way is really alive and strongly inspired. Think of a very high achiever's performance compared to an average person's; the difference is enormous. My point is not to argue for a specific value for each element but to illustrate that the mind is so much more powerful than the body and that the Spirit is so much more powerful than the mind. If you want to achieve something great in life, you must combine all three.

For example, let's look at an athlete. An athlete who uses only her body could score goals in the weekend pick-up game. However, a lot of athletes have strong physical skills, so an athlete using only her physical skills would not stand out in a crowd. But if the athlete uses her mind as well as her body, then she will be a much better player and maybe go on to lead her team to the state championship in high school. But to be a top performer, the athlete must also engage her Spirit to have the inspiration to perform at a high level. This might lead to an Olympic gold medal.

Everyone has the amazing gift of the Spirit. You can communicate with it through prayer. When you do, you receive:

- Belief that you're doing what God designed you to do

- Confidence in yourself and your abilities
- The faith that you can achieve what you set out to do
- Inspiration that gives you the unfathomable energy and burning desire to succeed
- Strength to develop and exercise self-discipline

FAITH

> *Faith is taking the first step even when You don't see the whole staircase.*
> **—Martin Luther King, Jr.**

One of the greatest motivators in my life has been faith that what I'm doing is God's will for me. This may sound strange, but when I was a child of about five, God spoke to me and told me that I was to be a teacher. I still remember that like it happened yesterday. Later, when I was a professor, I remembered that this was what God wanted me to do. Every day before class, I prayed that God would guide me to do His will and not let my ego get in the way. As a result, the classes that I taught were just amazing to me. My evaluations from students indicated they felt the same way. That was one place in life where I felt I was in the zone, like I was suspended from myself and was gliding along on God's power.

When students asked me questions, I would answer with an example that I had never thought of before and sometimes didn't know that I knew. But it would be the perfect example for the situation. I've not been blessed with a lot of patience, but in the classroom, I exhibited patience that astounded me.

Do you know what it is like to be operating in your purpose? An excellent example is seen in the movie *Billy Elliot* about a boy who wanted to be a ballet dancer but grew up in a coal mining town in England. At one point, Billy is asked what it's like when he dances. He responds that it's like he is somewhere else, like electricity is running through his body. When he dances, he's doing exactly what he was designed to do. He had to fight his family and neighborhood to do it, but he did it successfully. He also changed the people around him by showing them his faith in what he was doing. He showed others in his community with less belief in themselves what life could offer them.

Faith is belief in the unseen

Faith is belief in the unseen. Faith isn't just about God but about anything in your life that you can't see. The biggest unseen part of your life is your future. You can exercise your faith that you'll have the future you want and change the direction of your life to be much more fulfilling.

If you have faith that you'll be a successful athlete, teacher, parent, truck driver, or anything else, then you multiply your chances of success. If you have faith that you'll be a failure, an addict, a prisoner, or homeless, then you'll achieve that instead. Why not pick something wonderful to do with your life and then live by faith that you'll be successful at it?

Sometimes people are afraid to have faith in themselves or their future. They feel that they don't deserve success or that it will be impossible. Each of you is a child of God, who loves you and wants you to be happy, so you definitely deserve to have a successful future.

CONFIDENCE

Believe in yourself!
Have faith in your abilities!
Without confidence in your own powers
You cannot be successful or happy.
—Norman Vincent Peale

Confidence comes from knowing that God made you and is with you in all that you do. Spirit gives you self-confidence.

Suppose that you believe God made you a perfect human being and that God loves you and wants you to be happy more than anything else in the whole universe. Think of the self-image and self-confidence you would possess knowing that God made you and loves you no matter what you've ever done in your life. To me, the greatest message of the

Christian church is that God loves you eternally, and God forgives you for everything that you have ever done. Now that is a powerful message.

When I was struggling with my self-image, my therapist told me to write down positive affirmations and to repeat them daily to reprogram my mind. I did this, and it worked—my mind sent me positive messages instead of negative messages. But the mind is like a computer and simply does what it's told without emotion. Reprogramming my mind helped, but it was only part of the change that I needed.

Later, my therapist told me to imagine that God made me and that he wants me to be happy. He said to picture that when I was born, I was a perfect image of God. However, my parents (who were not perfect) raised me, and they unintentionally taught me that I was unworthy and unlovable. I had a choice: I could hold on to the beliefs that my parents taught me, or I could replace them with new beliefs. How wonderful it is to believe that I was created by God in his own image and that he wants me to be all that I can be. Let me tell you that once I changed my beliefs, my self-image changed radically, and my self-confidence went through the roof. If God loves me, then what does it matter what person thinks about me?

This is an example of how my subconscious mind was in conflict with my Spirit. The conflict lasted for many years in which I struggled to find peace. I knew that I had some kind of disturbance inside, but I didn't know what it was until my therapist helped me. Once I aligned my subconscious mind and my Spirit, my world changed dramatically.

INSPIRATION

> *Not all of us can do great things.*
> *But we can do small things*
> *With great love.*
> **—Mother Teresa**

Inspiration comes from your Spirit and gives you the confidence to act on your beliefs. Insecurity is the opposite of inspiration and certainly doesn't lead to much self-confidence. If you are insecure, you doubt your self-worth or your abilities, and you lack confidence to act on what's inside you. Insecurity causes people to look to things outside themselves to give their lives meaning and purpose. Unfortunately, because many parents don't know how to be good parents, they cause their children to be insecure and to lack the self-confidence to go out into the world on their own.

The most powerful aspect of all that the Spirit gives us is inspiration. A person who is inspired has tons of energy and drive. They have self-confidence, they believe that they're doing what they were designed to do, and they're practically guaranteed to be successful. Don't get in the way of an inspired person because there is no stopping him or her. Right or wrong, that person will succeed because of his certainty that what he's doing is what he was meant to do.

Inspiration plays a big part in finding your purpose in life. If you want to have a significant life, you can do all the research and soul searching in the world, but until you get truly inspired, you won't find your true purpose. Just think of the last time you did something that you were truly inspired to do. You forgot to eat. You forgot the time. You forgot other duties that you were supposed to do because you were just so lost in that activity that the rest of the world ceased to exist to you. When I go to the theater and paint sets, this happens to me. One day I was asked to paint a scene of a street in London. For about four hours, I was completely lost in the task, and absolutely nothing existed to me except what I was doing. Before I knew it, it was getting late, way past quitting time, and I hadn't eaten or even thought of eating during that time.

Those are the experiences of life that you never forget because you would like to get them back or to duplicate them in some way. I can remember some of those moments from earlier in my life. I hope you've had a lot of those moments in your life. You can tap into the power of inspiration and make it happen more often if you want. You just need to get in touch with your Spirit and communicate your desires to find what you were designed to do. Then you listen for the response.

It is important to listen to your Spirit because it will tell you what you were designed to do rather than what you want to do. You may want to have a great day kayaking tomorrow, but you may not get to do that because the Spirit tells you that you need to spend time with your sick child. If you ignore the Spirit and go kayaking, you may have a terrible time because you're not inspired. On the other hand, if you spend the time with your sick child, you may experience one of the greatest moments in your relationship. You never know when these special moments will come up.

PERSONAL GROWTH EXERCISE:

Describe how your Spirit works for you.

Does it give you hope?

_____
_____
_____

Does it give you a sense of self-worth?

_____
_____
_____

Does it give you self-confidence?
_____
_____
_____

Does it inspire you?
_____
_____
_____

> **PLEASE, STOP AND COMPLETE THIS WRITTEN EXERCISE BEFORE GOING ON!**
>
> **BE PART OF THE SUCCESSFUL 2 PERCENT AND COMPLETE THE EXERCISE NOW!**

SUMMARY

Your Spirit is a part of God living inside you. That means that you can directly communicate with God anytime you want to exercise that connection. If God is for you, who can be against you? Just think of that! If part of God lives inside of you, and God wants you to be successful in life, all you have to do is learn to be in tune with God to have a wonderful life.

Belief in yourself is critical to achieving anything in life. This self-confidence will allow you to try new things and grow. Visualization is a wonderful tool for seeing what you want to become.

Your Spirit is also the source of your motivation and inspiration so it is important to be in touch with what is happening in your Spirit.

Section Three:

LEARNING NEW HABITS

Chapter Nine

ROCKS TO DIAMONDS CYCLE

*You Should Always Pursue Perfection,
You Just Might Reach Excellence*
—Vince Lombardi

Change can be very threatening to some people. However, without change it is impossible to grow and improve. I understand that change involves risk, but doing nothing may involve even more risk. No matter what you do in the future, it involves risk.

Sometimes it is actually easier to change that to stay where you are.

In today's world of seemingly constant change, being flexible and adaptable are critical to survival as well as success. This chapter discusses how you successfully make change in your life.

FEEDBACK LOOP

This section talks about a simple process that you can use to make changes in your life. This process works in any part of life where repetition leads to success, such as learning to play the piano or learning to speak Spanish. This does not work well in situations that are one time only like a lawsuit. Anyone familiar with feedback loops will recognize those as the foundation of the *Rocks to Diamonds* Cycle. Rocks represent you in their raw state, before you've discovered and developed your gifts. Diamonds represent you after you have discovered and developed these gifts. Here are the four steps in the *Rocks to Diamonds* Cycle:

STEP 1:

Rocks represent your potential in life. You have lots of potential that you don't use. No matter what level you are performing at right now, you still have lots more untapped potential. Your body could perform at a much higher level than it does now. As was discussed earlier, you are not using the full capacity of your mind, and you are not engaging your Spirit nearly as much as you could.

STEP 2:

Effort is the action you take to use your potential to accomplish the task at hand. You apply your *body*, *mind*, and *Spirit* as well as you can at that point in your life. You choose how much effort you exert each day. Since it is your choice, why not choose to give it your all?

STEP 3:

Result is the outcome of the effort you applied to your potential. You might think that the more effort you apply, the better the result. However, both the quantity and the quality of the effort determine the outcome. You've heard the old expression "It is better to work smarter, not just harder."

STEP 4:

Belief refers to what you think about yourself and about your abilities. At step 2, you begin to believe in the result you'll get from step 3. After step 3 is complete, one of three things will happen: your belief in your ability to obtain the desired outcome will increase, decrease, or stay the same. Stay the same is an unlikely outcome in my opinion. If you apply yourself you will probably get better even if it is just a little tiny bit. If you don't apply yourself, then you will get worse even though it also might be just a tiny little bit.

REPEAT STEP 1:

Go back to *Rocks*, your potential. Now that you've had experience from going through the previous loop, you can change your performance. If your time through the loop was successful, your belief in your ability to obtain the desired outcome is now greater, and you will apply that new belief to your potential. Your potential hasn't changed but you now *believe* that you have more ability to use your potential than before. When you complete another loop, you should see greater results than the previous time because of this increased belief in yourself.

REPEAT STEP 2:

You will put forth better *effort* this time because now you are more confident that you will have success in your endeavors. Remember, since success breeds success, you need to challenge yourself to improve constantly. However, failure breeds failure, so if you had a bad result the first time, you will have to put forth more and/or better effort this time.

REPEAT STEP 3:

The *result* will probably be better than before: you're improving. This improvement may be only incremental, but as you complete the cycle more times, the increments add up to a significant improvement.

The 1% a Day Principle: if you improve your performance in some area by just 1% every day, in just 3 months you will have doubled your performance. While 1% a day sounds like such a small improvement, it is huge when done on a consistent basis.

Never give up!

REPEAT STEP 4:

Your *belief* in yourself will increase more and more as you see improvement. The ideal outcome is that your belief turns into certainty. Then, you will be performing at the highest level and you will truly be a "DIAMOND".

You can continue through the loop as many times as you want or need to. Hopefully, you get better every time you cycle through. There truly is no limit to your success. You might feel that you will reach a limit or know everything that there is to know, but that is simply not true. There is always something new to learn or a different way to do what you are doing. It seemed that I learned something new every day when I was teaching. Most of what I learned was from my students.

The *Rocks to Diamonds Cycle* applies to any situation where you learn through repetition. For example, if you're learning to play a musical instrument, you go through a cycle each time you practice or play. You need to monitor how much effort you're giving and how good that effort is, how the result changed, and how your belief in your ability improves with practice. The old saying "practice makes perfect" is wrong. The correct saying is, "perfect practice makes perfect." If you practice poorly, then you'll learn to play poorly. So each time you practice, you should plat like you are giving a great performance and always put forth your best effort.

You need to ensure that you do not become discouraged by setbacks. You must make sure that a bad day doesn't get you off track. A bad cycle doesn't reduce your potential; it should certainly not reduce the effort that you put forward or your belief in yourself. You must learn from the bad cycles and focus on the good cycles to avoid failure.

Success will broaden your life and lead to even greater success. Once you have experienced success in one area of life, it will give you more confidence in other areas. This will lead to greater success in those areas with less time and effort required to achieve it.

I apply this *Rocks to Diamond Cycle* to my life by choosing something and working on it for a period of time. I treat it like a short term project. After I have gone through several cycles and I can see the improvement, the process has now become a habit, a good habit. I will continue with that area of my life and then tackle another area. Rather than trying to make big changes to many areas of my life I change one area at a time. Just think of the results if you developed just

3 or 4 new good habits every year. Over 5 or 10 or 20 years, that would be a significantly better life.

Each of these steps will be discussed in more detail in the following chapters.

ROCKS TO DIAMONDS CYCLE

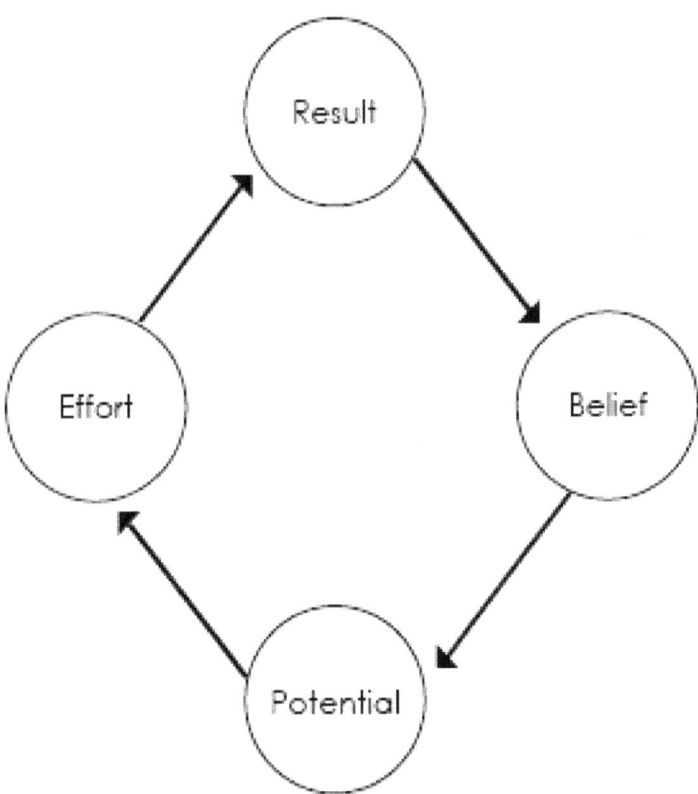

SUMMARY

When you take one hour a day and apply yourself to learning something new, you can use this *Rocks to Diamonds Cycle* to master what you're learning. The repetition leads to improvement. Some times the improvement may be small but over time the consistency of your effort will yield great results.

You can apply this *Rocks to Diamonds* method to almost any area of your life. However, this cycle applies to situations where there are a series of steps or loops involved. It would not apply to a one-time only event, such as a lawsuit or winning the lottery.

Chapter Ten

ROCKS = OUR POTENTIAL

*Impossible is not a fact,
It's an opinion.
Impossible is not a declaration,
It's a dare.
Impossible is potential.*
—Muhammad Ali

When I was a little boy I had big dreams but I believed that I didn't possess the ability to undertake them. I have since learned that every single person on earth has the potential to do amazing things.

You may not realize your potential because you don't understand just what you are capable of achieving. If you want to do something special, you have the potential to do it.

If you can imagine a better life or dream of success, then you are capable of achieving it.

MORE POTENTIAL THAN IMAGINABLE

I honestly believe that you miss so much in life because you don't understand the incredible potential you possess. To help you see your potential more clearly, review the following questions:

How do you see yourself?

- Worthless
- Not able to succeed
- Lacking potential

      OR

- Created by God
- Designed to be great
- Put on earth for a unique purpose

How do you spend your time?

- Working
- Watching television
- Existing

      OR

- Enjoying every incredible day
- Loving the people in your life
- Experiencing God's amazing creation

ROCKS = OUR POTENTIAL

How do you view other people?

- Boring
- Threatening
- A way to get what I want

    OR

- An opportunity to learn more
- An amazing heart
- A thrill to be around

How do you perceive the world around you?

- It's nice
- The weather is okay
- I wish I lived somewhere else

    OR

- Amazed at the beauty of each day
- Thrilled to be able to take a walk and enjoy the wonders of nature
- Inquisitive about how each part of creation fits together in such an awesome manner

Do you have any idea what your potential might be? I would say that no one knows his or her true potential because it's limitless. It's fun to learn about your potential. This is one of the reasons why I recommend that you set goals. Your periodic review of your goals will show your progress toward realizing your potential. Everyone starts out in life with a limited view of what they can do. All too often, that is based on what was done in the past. But what you did in the past will always be less than what you're capable of doing. You truly have unlimited potential inside of you, so if you use it, you can truly do almost anything that you want to do.

Do you know what a geode is? It is a rock that looks plain on the outside but has a beautiful crystalline interior. If you saw a pile of geodes, you probably wouldn't give them any special regard because they look like plain rocks. However, if you cut one open, you'd find the beauty on the inside.

You are like a geode. From the outside, you may appear plain, but once you look inside, you find that you are filled with a treasure of gifts and talents. Everyone is truly beautiful on the inside.

You really don't have any idea of your true potential. I remember being told that I would never make it in university by my high school teachers and counselors. What they saw was a troubled young man who had attitude problems. What they didn't see was that I had a lot of drive and ambition. Without channels for that drive and ambition, I was bored and frustrated. But, when I got a chance to use them later in life, I came alive and accomplished what I feel are

ROCKS = OUR POTENTIAL

great things. I still believe that the best is yet to come in my life.

Your potential is truly unlimited. You must find ways to use the potential you possess. Try new things all the time. Experiment with what you think you would like to do. Here is an excellent practice which I use. I continually look for things that are outside of my comfort zone. I then evaluate if I want to spend the time and effort to accomplish this. If the answer is yes, then I dedicate myself to learning and doing that thing until it is conquered.

Recently I was asked to organize a speech contest. Organizing anything is outside of my comfort zone. I have been primarily a sole performer all my life. But I considered if I wanted to be able to do this. The answer was yes. So I tackled it. The first few months I organized a special meeting of speakers with about six attendees. That went well so I organized a speech contest with about thirty attendees and that went well. Then I organized another with forty attendees. Now I am in the planning process for a conference with approximately two hundred attendees. By setting my goals and then working towards it one step at a time, I have found that the success of one step has increased my self-confidence going into the next step.

Don't just blindly follow what others tell you to do. Often they're talking from their limited experience with you, so they don't know what you could achieve if you were given the opportunity. No matter what you want to do, a whole tribe of people will tell you that you can't do it or that it can't be done. If you listen to them, you may find yourself not succeeding.

When I was a teenager, I wanted to move to California. I was told that it was impossible to get to California from Nova Scotia - not physically impossible, but impossible for someone like me who was performing at less than my potential. This would have been terribly limiting had I truly believed it. However, two people showed me that this wasn't true.

The first one was Denny Doherty, a member of the popular musical group *The Mamas and the Papas,* who was from Halifax. Not only had he made it to California, but he was also a member of one of the most popular musical groups of that time. The second happened when I was in grade ten. My homeroom teacher left during the school year to go to California to get married.

Despite the fact that people had said it was impossible to get from Nova Scotia to California, here were two people who contradicted that idea and allowed me to have hope of going there.

ROCKS = OUR POTENTIAL

When I was thirty years old, I moved to California and lived there for the next twenty-five years. So much for being impossible!

Until the sixteenth century, people believed that the earth was the center of the solar system until Copernicus wrote that the sun was the center of the solar system.

Christopher Columbus set sail on his remarkable voyage to find a westward passage to the East. It is worth noting that Columbus was a failure in that he did not do what he set out to do, yet he is regarded as one of the great explorers in the history of the world. Why did he achieve success? Because he set out to do something! He had a goal and took action to achieve it.

Many people believed that heavier-than-air flight was impossible until the Wright brothers did it.

A large number of people believed that a man of color could not get elected president of the United States until Barack Obama went out and did it.

We can look at history and see case after case of people going against the grain and achieving the "impossible". You have great potential within you; you just have to find a way to use it and to achieve your goals.

Not everyone has the same potential. God gives each of us a unique set of gifts and talents that you need for your specific purpose. It is necessary for you to find out what that special purpose is and to go after it.

GIFTS AND TALENTS

When you were born, you already possessed your unique gifts and talents. Unfortunately, you must find out for yourself what those gifts and talents are to be truly happy. I believe that you can find contentment in a career by using one of these skills, but you won't realize your full potential for joy and happiness until you discover what your real gifts and talents are and develop them.

You will be successful when you're doing what you were designed to do. That means that it is important that you discover your gifts and talents and then develop them.

I was very lucky because God told me as a little boy that I was to be a teacher, giving me a sense of purpose in life. I never doubted that it would happen or that I would be able to do it. Even though in my twenties I knew nothing I could teach anyone and was so introverted that I couldn't talk to two people without getting flustered, I persevered. Just like magic, the doors in life opened to me and finally led me to be a professor at age twenty-nine. The first time I stepped into a classroom, I loved it and had that feeling of being off in another world. By being persistent, I was ready when the opportunities were presented to me.

During my career, I was often offered better paying jobs with more prestige, but I never for one minute considered accepting any of them. I was doing what I was designed to do, so it would have been foolish to change my career. If you are truly happy with your job, it is probably not because of the money but because you are utilizing your gifts and talents. Conversely, if you are unhappy with your job, it is probably not because of the money but because you are not able to fully use your gifts and talents.

There is an old saying, *"Choose a job you love and you will never have to work a day in your life."*

LIFE EXPERIENCES

You learn not only from formal education but also from life experiences. What you learn from life can be positive or negative, depending on what experiences you have. You may have learned lessons that were completely compatible with your gifts and talents. These experiences helped you develop them and prepared you for using them. On the other hand, your life experiences may have blocked your gifts and talents. These may have actually prevented you from discovering and developing them.

Parents are a great influence. As your primary caregivers for the first part of your life, what they teach you is very significant and will last a lifetime for many people. If you had loving parents, then you likely developed a strong sense of self-worth. If they exposed you to many different sports, hobbies, activities, and educational experiences, then you had a greater chance of discovering what your gifts and talents were at a young age. These positive life experiences make it easier for you to realize your potential.

However, if your parents were ill equipped to be parents, then your life experiences may not have been so encouraging. If your parents were unable to love you because of their own unfortunate dysfunction, then your parents would not have been able to give you a strong sense of self-worth. In fact, the opposite may have happened: they may have given you a negative sense of self-worth that would make achieving any success more difficult. If they weren't effective parents, then you may have had a difficult time discovering and developing your gifts and talents.

But the picture is not all bleak for those of you who didn't have the Super Parents. I believe my parents' poor parenting is a major source of my strength today. My father was seldom sober, and my mother was so preoccupied with him that I ended up being neglected as a child. I was often told to do something but given no parental help or supervision.

I learned to be very resourceful and to do things by myself. I have a great sense of self-discipline that I feel developed because of the situation in my childhood home.

I also learned to be independent, which meant that I could survive adversity and be confident that I would make it. As an adult, I went through divorce and emigration to another country with no family support of any kind. Also, my situation at home motivated me to become successful so I wouldn't end up like my dad. (I feel that my dad wasted his life through his use excessive of alcohol.) That meant getting an education, which has made all the difference in my life. The motivational speaker, Wayne Dyer, experienced similar circumstances in his childhood. His father's abandonment of the family led him to learn self-reliance. That is a major theme of his philosophy of life.

Individuals with great parents can turn out to be unsuccessful in life. On the other hand, many people who had bad childhoods and seem to have everything going against them can become hugely successful in life. *It is not your situation that determines your success as much as your response to the situation.*

It is not your situation that determines your success as much as your response to the situation.

If you look at two people who grew up in the same bad environment, you might see that they had very different responses to the situation. One responds by refusing to let the hardships destroy his life. He becomes determined to succeed in life. The other person growing up in the same household gives up and becomes an alcoholic, feeling sorry for himself because of what happened during his childhood.

You must never live in the past!

You must never live in the future!

You must always live in the present!

In other words, what happened to you in your past need not control your present. What might or might not happen in the future should not affect what you do today, unless of course, you can predict that your actions will have direct consequences. You shouldn't live today in fear that in the future something bad might happen, such as getting cancer. However, you shouldn't go out and rob a bank today feeling that what happens tomorrow doesn't matter.

You must live in the present while keeping in mind that your actions today may affect the future. You must always live in the present because it is the only time when you have any power to make choices and take action. You are responsible for your future. Your decisions today will determine you're your future success and happiness.

DISCOVERING YOUR UNIQUE TALENT

A real problem for many people is discovering their true gifts and talents. Often people haven't spent much time trying to figure this out. Usually they are so busy going and doing in today's society that they don't stop and contemplate. In this age of electronics, people are often involved with some form of communication or entertainment device. Many people just don't take the time to think.

While driving in the car, you have time to contemplate life and your future. When you go for a walk or do your daily exercise you have time to use your mind for reflection. Every day there are opportunities to think about the purpose of your time spent here on earth.

Discovering your talents requires that you take some time to stop and contemplate your life. Doing so may mean reading books and doing some exercises to determine what your gifts are. Whatever method you use, you need to take definite action toward discovering your gifts and talents.

One approach is to think of what has made you extremely happy in the past. Another is to talk to family members, friends, and teachers and ask them what they think your gifts and talents might be. A third method is to review what types of work you have done and see what you were very good at.

Unfortunately, there is no easy answer to finding your gifts and talents. The two methods that I would recommend above all the others are prayer and meditation. Your subconscious mind and your Spirit may have the answer. If you pray, you are asking your Spirit what you want to know. At the same time your subconscious mind picks up what you are looking for. When you meditate you are listening to your subconscious mind and your Spirit. You should pray and meditate until you receive the answer.

MEANING AND PURPOSE IN LIFE

Sometimes you find meaning and purpose from unusual circumstances. If you are open and seeking them, you will find them. I once had a student named Aimee who was doing okay with her studies but never knew where she was going for a career. During her junior year, her grandmother in Virginia had a bad fall and suffered serious injuries. Since Aimee was close to her grandmother and seeing that no one else in the family was able to go to the grandmother's home to help her, Aimee volunteered to take time from her studies and help her grandmother.

Aimee spent three months nursing her grandmother back to health. When she returned to school, she came to see me and tell me that she was changing her major. I hardly recognized her because she had changed from a low energy, unmotivated person into a very energetic, highly motivated person. She said that the time with her grandmother had shown her what her true purpose was, and she decided to switch her major from business to nursing. The last time I heard from Aimee, she was happily involved in a career in nursing.

When you feel that your life lacks meaning, you need to determine what your true purpose is in life. You want to find a purpose that will give you a sense of significance. However, you can't find your sense of purpose until you have determined what your gifts and talents are. *Purpose in life is simply using your gifts and talents as they were meant to be used.*

> Purpose in life is simply using your gifts and talents as they were meant to be used

My gift is teaching. When I talk in front of a group I feel completely content and in my element. I feel that this is what I should be doing. I guess you could say that this is when I feel closest to God because I know that I'm doing exactly what He designed me to do.

It may be difficult and it may take some time, but when you find the thing that you were designed to do, your whole life shifts and you'll have more inner joy and peace. No one has to tell you when that happens. You will know before anyone else does.

I believe that the two greatest days in your life are the day you were born and the day you discovered why!

PERSONAL GROWTH EXERCISE:

What are your gifts and talents in life?

_____
_____
_____

What special skills were you born with?

_____
_____
_____

What interests do you have?

_____
_____
_____

What abilities do you have?

_____
_____
_____

What are you good at?

_____
_____
_____

> **PLEASE, STOP AND COMPLETE THIS WRITTEN EXERCISE BEFORE GOING ON!**
>
> **BE PART OF THE SUCCESSFUL 2 PERCENT AND COMPLETE THE EXERCISE NOW!**

I believe that the two greatest days in your life are; the day you were born and the day you discovered why

SUMMARY

It would be interesting if there was a way to measure your potential. If it was just like your bathroom scales, you could just step on it and find your real potential. You would be truly amazed at what you could do. Since there is no way to measure what your potential is, you must work throughout your life assuming that you are not reaching the limits of your potential. The more that you use your gifts and talents; the more your potential seems to grow.

Your potential is your gifts and talents. These were inside you when you were born. The problem is that no one ever tells you what they are. You must find them for yourself and that can be a life long process. Often you think you have discovered your gifts and talents but you are only part way there. I believe that you could always be expanding the use of your gifts and talents your whole life long.

Once you have found your gifts and talents and start to use them and develop them, then your life will take on meaning and a sense of purpose. This is ultimate happiness.

Chapter Eleven

EFFORT = USING YOUR POTENTIAL

*Continuous effort is the key
To unlocking your potential*
—Winston S. Churchill

It is easy to fall into complacency in life. Life is pretty good so why work to improve. You are happy where you are, why should you risk what you have? Life can always be better and much more rewarding. You should not let your fears limit your life.

The more you grow, the more you see what you can achieve. To be happy at the highest levels, you need to be working towards your true purpose in life. You will never know what that is until you truly apply yourself to using your potential to its fullest. While this involves risk, remember that everything in life involves risk in one way or another. The opportunity not taken could have as much risk as the opportunity taken.

THE LEGACY OF BUDDY HOLLY

Why is it that some people apply so much effort to what they do? I visited the Buddy Holly museum in Lubbock, Texas and was amazed by how much influence he had on other performers. Although you may not know who Buddy Holly was, you probably have seen and heard the results of his influence. Buddy Holly was a rock and roll pioneer back in the 1950's. He died in a plane crash on February 3, 1959, at the age of only twenty-two. During his short life, he was a dedicated musician. At the age of twelve he discovered a talent for playing the guitar. He was completely absorbed with playing and writing music and experimenting with rock 'n' roll.

He spent virtually every minute of every day on his music. The effort he exerted wasn't hardship or work because he did it for the love of music. He applied his effort completely to his music.

Who was influenced by Buddy Holly's efforts?

- He established the model for rock 'n' roll bands that has been used for the past fifty years
- The first forty songs by the Beatles were heavily influenced by his work

- The Rolling Stones, the Hollies, Peter and Gordon, and many other groups of the 1960s and later were influenced by him
- Elton John, who is famous for wearing outlandish eyeglasses, first wore them to imitate Buddy Holly

If you apply effort to your potential, you will have an influence way beyond anything that you can imagine

If you apply effort to your potential, you will have an influence way beyond anything that you can imagine. As you see with Buddy Holly, you don't have to have a long career to influence people.

APPLYING EFFORT IS YOUR CHOICE

I wasted my teenage years because I was filled with bitterness and resentment. For years I told myself that it wasn't my fault and that I didn't deserve it. I should have had a better childhood like all the other kids. I believed it was my dad's fault and that I was just an innocent bystander. While I may have been correct, that attitude did me no good. But I've come to realize that my response to my home life was *my* responsibility. I chose to feel the way I did. That was a difficult truth for me to accept.

As I've mentioned before, I grew up in a dysfunctional home with an alcoholic father and a mother who was distracted by my dad's drinking. "Poor me, no one loves me" was my attitude in childhood and it carried over into my adult years also.

Out of that experience grew bitterness, and out of bitterness grew resentment. When I first started my personal growth, I looked back and realized that I never worried about the future. I wasn't afraid of life. I didn't have many of the fears that I saw in people around me. Instead, the predominant emotion of my life had been resentment toward my parents. During my teenage years, because of the pain I felt, I often experienced two conflicting options for the future: one was running away and the other was suicide. Fortunately, I did not do either one.

Someone with this attitude doesn't experience life positively. My bad attitude led me to not apply myself at school and to withdraw from friends and family and to develop some bad habits. I wasn't a discipline problem and rebellious, but I was the opposite - I withdrew from life and tried to be invisible. Plain and simple, I had a bad attitude. I was like a car in neutral; I had no drive to live my life each day.

This affected my development. I basically stopped growing emotionally at age fourteen and didn't start again until I started therapy at age forty. Please don't be like me and waste a portion of your life. It's important that you not waste one single day, one single hour, or one single minute living in the past because no matter how hard you try, *you cannot change your past.*

Amazingly, looking at my past today I see that I was very lucky in many ways. One is that I did not get involved with drugs or alcohol. So many youth of that generation and today get involved in activities that permanently affect my life. Despite my dad's problems, he was adamant that I get an education. That was my way out of the life I was living.

One of the big breakthroughs in my therapy was forgiving my parents. I was living in the past by holding on to the anger and resentment that I felt for my parent's dysfunctional behavior. I could never focus on the current events in my life because I was always stuck in the past. However, once I forgave my parents, I was freed from the past and was able to live more in the present moment. It was a huge change in my life.

How can you forgive someone? I worked at it in therapy and with a lot of prayer. One day I suddenly saw the situation differently. Instead of focusing on me and my pain, I focused on my parents and their pain. Like me, they grew up in dysfunctional homes and were doing the best job that they could. Their bad parenting wasn't malicious, just a product of their own childhoods. This made forgiving them much easier. Forgiving is truly freeing. When we forgive someone else, we are truly the ones who benefit because we no longer have to live with these negative feelings. Often the other person doesn't even know how you feel about him or her.

If you have read the book "*The Four Agreements*" by Don Miguel Ruiz you will know that one of his agreements is "*Don't take anything personally*". That is what I had done. I had assumed that my parent's treatment of me was because of me and that I was unlovable. In reality, it was because of themselves and the fact that they were incapable of loving me because of their own problems.

The only time in which you have any power is the present. You can't change the past or what you experienced. You can't live in the future because it is not guaranteed to anyone. You can only live in the present. Therefore, forgive anyone in your past who you feel has harmed you in any way. Let go of that negative energy in your body and be free from all those bad feelings.

I have heard it said that "Un-forgiveness is like taking poison and waiting for the other person to die". The only person who is affected by un-forgiveness is you. Forgiveness is a blessing on you. It is not releasing the other person from what they did but releasing you from the memory of what they did.

You need to live today to the maximum. You must completely apply yourself to everything that you do. When I get up in the morning, I often exercise first thing while listening to a motivational CD. I'm fully present and experience my exercise as exhilarating. It sets a great mood for the day. When I run, I love the time. I enjoy feeling the strain, managing my breathing, watching the sky and the weather, and just being alone in God's wonderful creation.

Every morning I do devotionals that include reading my Bible, reading inspirational materials, and praying about my day and what's going on in my life.

Whatever I do during the day, whether it is work, volunteering, spending time with friends, or hiking in nature, I try to be 100 % present and aware of my life every minute. I don't want to waste one more day of my life with a bad attitude.

Despite how you may feel, life on earth is short so you must learn to live every moment to the fullest.

GOALS

Goals are an important part of effort. They will determine what effort you give, when you give it, and how you give it. Your effort is much more effective if you focus it on a single goal or a small group of goals. Look at the sun's rays as an example. Sunlight hits the surface of the earth and warms it. If you take that sunlight and focus it through a magnifying glass, that same sunlight can start a fire.

You can apply effort to carry out your potential for a certain effect. But, as with the magnifying glass, if you focus that effort on your goals, you'll magnify your power and achieve much greater results. *By focusing your effort on the proper goals, you'll progress more rapidly and achieve results beyond your expectations.*

I can't say enough about the importance of goals in your life. I see people every day who have no formal goals and are just living in a meaningless existence. On the other hand I see people every day who are living with goals and are happy and excited about every day. Even bad days are good for someone with goals because even bad days are getting them towards their goals.

If you don't know where to start, let me give you a suggestion. Find a Toastmasters club in your area and commit to completing your Competent Communicator in one year. I guarantee it will change your life. It will get you out of your comfort zone and moving forward. During that year I believe that you will get motivated and start doing other great things with your life.

MOTIVATION

I would like you to do an exercise about motivation. Pretend you are going for a nice walk. Take a few minutes and close your eyes and take a walk. Please stop reading and do this exercise for two minutes.

> *STOP! STOP READING AND TAKE A WALK.*
>
> *IF YOU CAN'T ACTUALLY TAKE A WALK, THEN JUST DO THE EXERCISE IN YOUR MIND!*
>
> *WHEN YOU FINISH YOUR WALK, TURN THE PAGE.*

Think about and write down what went through your mind on your walk.

_____
_____
_____
_____

Were you wondering:

> Where am I supposed to be?
>
> Where am I supposed to be going?
>
> How far am I supposed to walk?
>
> What am I supposed to be doing as I walk?

Most people like structure in their lives. They want to know where they're going, how long it'll take to get there, and why they're going somewhere. Unfortunately, having these answers may lead to problems:

1. You may think only in the short term, as it is easier to achieve the certainty that you crave.
2. You may listen to what others tell you about how to lead your life.
3. You may not accomplish half of what you are capable of doing.
4. You may go in the wrong direction for you.

EFFORT = USING YOUR POTENTIAL

Since many people don't know how to plan their own lives (after all, when were they taught that?), they don't have a plan and are all too willing to live without long-term goals or to accept what someone else tells them. Notice that the questions that I thought you might have during the walk all contained "supposed to." This implies you desired someone to tell you what to do instead of figuring it out for yourself.

There is a great scene in the movie *The Dead Poets Society* when the professor takes the students to an outdoor plaza and tells them to walk around; he gives them no other rules or directions. At first everyone is bewildered that they have been told to do something without specific directions and they're tentative about walking. But slowly, each person starts doing something different. This feels uncomfortable for many students, and soon they start following the patterns of others rather than their inner selves.

When my students asked me which careers they should choose, I often got the feeling that they didn't want my opinion to throw in with the other opinions to ponder. Instead, I felt they wanted me to tell them which career to choose and the five steps to get there.

Fortunately for them, I didn't give them specific answers. I probed to find out what they wanted to do and what they were good at. I asked them what they dreamed of doing if there were no limits. Then I would encourage them to follow their dreams even if they thought it was impossible or unlikely that they could that.

A plan is a wonderful motivator. For example, my plan was to write this book. As I wrote, I became completely focused on it. When I read or talked to people, my mind always related ideas back to the book:

"That is a great point! Where could I use it?"

"That could be a chapter title!"

"That is a great quote!"

"I could incorporate that idea into my book."

I teach public speaking because I believe that the ability to speak in public is important to success. Public speaking will give you not only the ability to speak to a group of people but also good leadership skills and above all else, self-confidence.

It was funny when I gave my students a speaking assignment. If I gave them specific directions, they moaned and groaned but accepted them and asked very few questions. However, if I gave them an assignment for a three-minute speech with no guidelines or no rules to follow, the questions came fast and furious. It wasn't unusual for a student to approach me on campus outside of class with a question. They would reluctantly follow the rules but had difficulty accepting complete freedom to do anything they desired.

It's human nature to want a certain degree of structure. Humans are wired that way. That's one reason you can accomplish more by having goals: they provide us with structure. However, if you want to achieve things in life you have to learn to live with a degree of uncertainty. If you are doing new things and living outside your comfort zone, you may feel a little uneasy. After a while you will see that the uneasy feeling is really excitement. You are experiencing and mastering new skills in life.

It is extremely important that you make *your own* plan. You should spend time setting goals as discussed earlier. You must make your own goals and not just accept what someone else tells you. Setting goals may take some time and effort, but it will pay off in the long run. A life lived with purpose will give you a life of significance, and you will enjoy living much more.

TIME

The three most important elements to manage are cash, time and attitude. Time is the most important by far. Here are a few reasons why:

1. You have a limited amount of time. No matter what you do, there is no way to extend the amount of time you have in your life.
2. Attitude is flexible and can be changed fairly easily.
3. There is unlimited cash available for you to use. A good idea will attract cash.

In today's world people seem to be in such a hurry to get where they're going that they don't really stop and think about why they are going there in the first place.

Just think of dating and marriage. Many people are so anxious to get married that they rush through the dating process and don't really enjoy the magic of getting to know the other person. Dating should be like a long slow dance. Too often people rush through the dating stage to get to the wedding but then end up divorced because they didn't lay the proper foundation in the dating stage. There is a big difference between a wedding and a marriage. The fairy tale ending of a wedding and "they lived happily ever after" is not the reality of today. A successful marriage is much more difficult than a wedding.

You may be thinking about an apparent contradiction when I speak of living in the present but also setting goals. How can you live in the present but work toward your goals for the future? When I say live in the present, I mean that you want to appreciate and do your best in every moment. You don't want to be absorbed with what happened in the past or worried about what will happen in the future. You want your mind to be present at all times. By working toward your goals you are making decisions in the present that will also lead to a wonderful future.

EFFORT = USING YOUR POTENTIAL

While you can't ignore your future, you want to make sure that you don't live in it. The most common way people live in the future is to worry about it. But just remember that most of the things that you worried about never happened.

Happiness or success happens when you're absorbed in working toward your goals. That means living in the present but also planning for and doing other work that will benefit your future. The great American writer, Edith Wharton, said that *"If only we'd stop trying to be happy, we could have a pretty good time."* This means that if you're only focused on your happiness, you'll have trouble being happy. Also, when people chase happiness itself, they too often take shortcuts such as using drugs and alcohol that prove not to work in the long term. Instead, happiness is a by-product of pursuing your goals.

I have observed that people who are busy with life are often happier than those who are looking for happiness. For example, I have seen friends who don't think about happiness, they just get absorbed in their work and are happy doing it. They're not looking for happiness; it just happens as a by-product of their work. On the other hand, I pursued happiness in my life. I was very aware of how unhappy I was. Instead of seeking happiness, I needed to pursue my goals using my God-given gifts. Happiness came when I forgot about being happy and started living my life with purpose.

You always need to keep your goals in mind and work toward them in the present. If you don't work toward your goals, your next present moments may not be so enjoyable.

You can live in the present and completely ignore the future but that is not a good idea. For example, if you commit a crime to satisfy a current desire, you may spend a lot of your future unhappy because of the consequences of your actions. A criminal will do something wrong today completely ignoring the fact that he might get caught. This is very short term and misguided thinking. But after talking with a few criminal lawyers I found that most criminals use very short term thinking which is why they get caught and end up in prison.

Most people don't commit crimes because they realize that there will be consequences in the future. Crime is an example of living in the present but harming the future. Instead, *your actions in the present must be consistent with your goals for the future.*

> Your actions in the present must be consistent with your goals for the future

PERSONAL GROWTH EXERCISE:

Here is an exercise to help put time into perspective. Answer the following short questions:

EFFORT = USING YOUR POTENTIAL

Who is your hero? _____

Why? _____

Does your hero live in the past, present or future? _____

What are your hero's goals?

_____
_____
_____

How many hours in the day does my hero have? _____

The purpose of this exercise is to get you to realize that your hero has the same number of hours in a day as you do. If your hero can accomplish so much, then you can also. You may not have the same skills and be able to do the same things as your hero, but you could accomplish as much in your field of expertise using your talents. I believe that you will find that your hero is a person who is very focused on just a few goals and spends a great deal of his time and effort working towards those goals. Your hero probably doesn't spend the majority of his time in unproductive activities.

PLEASE, STOP AND COMPLETE THIS WRITTEN EXERCISE BEFORE GOING ON!

BE PART OF THE SUCCESSFUL 2 PERCENT AND COMPLETE THE EXERCISE NOW!

TYPES OF EFFORT

The three types of effort are:

- Physical
- Mental
- Spiritual

The body, mind, and Spirit also show you the three types of effort that you can use. The effort you use will vary depending on the situation. But there is seldom a situation that requires a single type of effort. You usually need a balance of the three.

Let's look at an example. When you study for a big exam, what type of effort do you use? Mental effort! But you don't use mental effort alone. You'll be much more successful if you incorporate physical effort to stimulate your mind, reduce stress, stay awake when studying, and sleep better the night before the exam. You must also include Spiritual effort for the motivation to succeed and the belief that you are worthy of the success.

The three types of effort are in a hierarchy of power. Physical effort is the most limited, and used alone, it will yield the most limited results. However, mental effort is almost unlimited and will multiply your physical effort and therefore the results that you achieve. Spiritual energy is beyond anything that you can imagine. If you engage Spiritual effort, hold on, because you'll probably go places and do things that you never dreamed were possible.

Let's see how this applies to a simple activity like picking up a heavy object. If you exert only physical effort, you'll simply bend over and pick the object up, or try to pick it up. This may work fine, but it may not work if the object is too heavy for you.

If you are having trouble lifting the heavy object, you could apply some mental effort and think:

"How else could I do this to get a better result?"

The answer will come if you give yourself a few minutes to engage your mind and tap into your subconscious. If it is a bigger problem it may take days or weeks but eventually you will get a better solution. The solution may be as simple as using a lever or pulley or it may be more complicated. No matter what the solution, some thought as to how to do it better will make picking up the object much easier.

Finally, if you apply Spiritual effort, you are almost unlimited in what you can do. Think of a story about a mother who picks up a car that has fallen on her child when normally she wouldn't have the physical strength. She doesn't have time to use mental effort; she has to act immediately. She is just so motivated by the thought of her child being crushed by the car that she does an amazing act. There is only one explanation for her strength; she uses Spiritual effort to accomplish this amazing feat.

You need to use all three types of effort in every situation. Using all three together will make the process easier and will allow you to accomplish much more.

I firmly believe that humans limit what they think they can achieve. They shortchange themselves when they limit their thinking or use negative thinking and say, "I can't." I believe that "I can't" means that "I didn't try hard enough".

I remember a time when I talked to a student about this. She doubted what I said was true. I told her she could do almost anything that she wanted to do, but she told me that the idea was stupid. She exclaimed with some delight (since she thought that she had proved me wrong):

"Well, I can't fly!"

I pointed out to her that there were several airports in the Bay Area from which she could fly anywhere in the world if she wanted. *You can accomplish almost anything, but sometimes you must shift the way you think.*

This is an example of the limits you might place upon yourself. You might immediately think of what you can't do. I've told other people they can do almost anything, and they have a response similar to my student. They'll try to think of the *one* situation in which they can't do it, and so they won't try.

EFFORT = USING YOUR POTENTIAL

If you say that you can't do something, then you have certainty in your world. However, if you suspend these thoughts, you can think of the possibility of doing it and then you have uncertainty. This is very uncomfortable for many people. I know that there have been circumstances in my life when I made bad decisions. Afterward, I wondered why I had done something that was against what I believed. Often it was because I couldn't stand the uncertainty of the moment. I decided in favor of the choice that gave me certainty and not the choice that gave me the best result.

One of the worst examples was an investment I made. I had saved up some money and wanted to invest it in a business. After I started searching for an investment, I got anxious because I found so many businesses to buy, but I didn't know much about most of them. My anxiety caused me to proceed too quickly and invest in a business that I knew nothing about. I lost all my money within a year. If I hadn't been so anxious and taken my time, I probably would have realized that investing in a business wasn't the best thing for me at that time.

You need to think differently in this area. Instead of looking for the one example where what you want to do won't work, you need to look for the one example where it might work. Once you see the one way it might work, then you will see even more possibilities. This is a powerful tool.

If you look at Roger Bannister, the first person to run a mile in less than four minutes, you see a fine example. Until 1954 when he broke the record, most people believed that it was impossible for a human to run a mile in less than four minutes. In fact scientists said that it was impossible for the human body. Bannister was running just over the four minute mark and believed that with more training he could break the record. That is exactly what he did because he believed that he could.

Here is the important lesson in this situation. The year after he ran the sub four minute mile, dozens of other runners did it also. As soon as people believed that it was possible, they were able to do it. The only thing that had changed was their belief about the four minute mile.

It seems that once people get thinking in one direction, they just continue in that way. This thinking is like being on railway tracks in that once they start on them they can only go where the tracks take them. This can be in the right or wrong direction as seen in the following spirals:

SPIRAL 1:

    Positive thinking breeds success!
    Success breeds more success!
    Success breeds positive thinking!
    Positive thinking breeds success!

EFFORT = USING YOUR POTENTIAL

SPIRAL 2:

> Negative thinking breeds failure!
> Failure breeds more failure!
> Failure breeds negative thinking!
> Negative thinking breeds failure!

One of these spirals goes up and the other goes down. Which one do you choose? That choice is completely up to you and no one else in the world. After all, you control your thoughts.

Compare the world today to the world of one hundred years ago. Many people of that day would have said that the computers, cars, planes, phones, televisions, and other forms of technology that we take for granted today would have been impossible. If everyone believed that, they would never have gone out and discovered or developed all these amazing inventions. *Without belief in success, you cannot venture into the unknown.*

> *Without belief in success, you cannot venture into the unknown*

Your beliefs about what you can and cannot do are an important part of your effort to succeed. These beliefs will determine the effort you put forth.

PERSONAL GROWTH EXERCISE:

Think of a time when you had to complete a difficult task. What kind of effort did you apply to complete the task?

_____
_____
_____

Think of a time when you had to complete an easy task. What kind of effort did you apply to complete the task?

_____
_____
_____

Describe a creative activity in which you were so wrapped up that you lost all track of time.

_____
_____
_____

How did you feel?

_____
_____
_____

Describe a routine activity that you thought was boring and you didn't really want to do but had to anyway.

_____
_____
_____

How did you feel?

_____
_____
_____

> **PLEASE, STOP AND COMPLETE THIS WRITTEN EXERCISE BEFORE GOING ON!**
>
> **BE PART OF THE SUCCESSFUL 2 PERCENT AND COMPLETE THE EXERCISE NOW!**

RISK FREE LIVING

There is no such thing as risk free living. People often make choices that they believe will give them a risk free life but it doesn't work. People stay working at a job they dislike because it is "secure" or has "good benefits". The truth is nothing is secure especially in the volatile economy of today.

Trying to live without risk has more to do with fear. In her wonderful book *"Feel the Fear...and Do It Anyway"*, Susan Jeffers shows how to recognize the fear that is felt in a certain situation but to go ahead and strive toward your goal anyway.

Regrets are a funny thing. Most people regret the things that they didn't do more than the things which they did. If you avoid doing something because of fear, it could lead to a lot of regrets later in your life, often soon after the event didn't happen.

On thing that people often don't do because of fear is "ask" for something. Men don't ask for a date because of fear. A salesperson doesn't ask the customer for the sale because of fear. A woman who is being mistreated by her husband doesn't ask him to stop out of fear. In there book "The Aladdin Factor", Jack Canfield and Mark Victor Hansen do an excellent job of showing you how to handle this problem.

Risk is an inherent part of life. Taking foolish risks may not be wise but also taking no risk is not wise either. It is necessary to balance the risks and rewards and decide what you want to do.

Here is a common story about avoiding risk. A person is in a job which they dislike. They are unwilling to leave the job because of their fear of risk. Then one day the choice is taken out of their hands, they get laid off for some reason. After a period of struggle when they figured out what they really wanted to do (since now that is a possibility), they started a business or new career and were hugely successful. They look back and are grateful for getting laid off because it was the key to changing their lives. It removed the fear of getting laid off out of the equation.

SUMMARY

You get to choose which effort to use every time you do something. If you make poor choices or apply too little effort, you get a poor result. However, if you choose to do your best and use all three types of effort - mind, body, and Spirit - the results are often surprising.

Looking to others is a great way to see what applying effort can do. Buddy Holly is only one individual who has inspired me by showing me what one person can do during a short period of time if he is truly committed to his purpose in life.

Motivation is an important part of effort because it points us in the right direction. You can achieve great things in life if you are going in the right direction and are applying your best effort.

Time is an interesting concept to understand. Sometimes it seems like there is so much and at other times it seems like there is so little. The truth is you have a limited amount of time on earth. It is important that you use your time wisely. I don't mean that you should be driven madly to achieve your goals but I certainly feel that you should be striving all the time towards them.

Finally, effort can be physical, mental or Spiritual but it is best when it is a balance of the three.

Chapter Twelve

RESULT = BENEFIT OF OUR EFFORT

*Happiness is not a goal;
It's a by-product of a life well lived.*
—**Eleanor Roosevelt**

What you can achieve is phenomenal. Do you feel that you have reached your peak today? If not, why not? I know that you have fantastic potential and that if you apply yourself, you will be amazed at what you can accomplish.

Life is short and is to be lived to the fullest. You only get once to live your life so why not live it to the fullest. If you want better relationships, a better career or better peace of mind, go after them with everything you possess. You are the only one who can make them come true for you.

VISION OF SUCCESS

What is your vision? Did this cycle get you closer to your vision? Once you have completed your effort, you need to assess the result in relation to your vision. It was important that you had a goal or plan before you started so that you know if you have accomplished what you set out to do. This will give you a standard or benchmark with which to compare your result.

Let us say that you are trying to lose weight. You goal is to reduce your weight from 190 to 150 pounds. After your first month you check your weight it is 185 pounds. Are you successful? You are successful in that you are making progress towards your big goal. You feedback is that what you did in the first month is working so keep it up.

If it was me, I would use the goal sequencing that we talked about in chapter 4. By this I would say my goals were to weigh:

Current 190
End of month 1 – 185
End of month 2 – 180
End of month 3 – 175
End of month 4 – 170
End of month 5 – 165
End of month 6 – 160
End of month 7 – 155
End of month 8 – 150

By using goal sequencing it would seem easier to be losing 5 pounds a month instead of 40 pounds all at once.

Maybe you never reach 150 pounds. Maybe you get down to 160 and just can't seem to get past that. Have you failed? If you look at the 150 you may feel that you failed. However, if you look at 190 you are certainly in a much better place than you were.

It is better to have a high goal and fall short than to have a low goal and achieve it.

It is better to have a high goal and fall short than to have a low goal and achieve it

What if your goal was to earn $1,000,000 and you earned only $900,000 did you fail? Once again if you look at the $1,000,000 you failed but if you look at the starting point you are doing very well.

The vision that you hold when you start our activity will determine how successful you feel once it is complete.

I volunteer at a local theater designing, building and painting sets for plays. I just love doing it. I enjoy it so much that I get lost in the process and become totally absorbed and happy. In building the sets, the crew's motto is, "We're not building a piano." In other words, we build a set to look nice for seven weeks while the play is running and then will be torn down. This of course is opposite to how a piano is made with lots of fabulous craftsmanship so that it plays well for decades or centuries. Our vision is a set that looks good, is safe, is strong enough to stay up for seven weeks but is easy to take down when we're finished with it. I hope that the piano maker's vision would be much different than that.

When you have a very definite vision of what you want to do, the task is easier to do, and you are better able to tell when you're finished. Writing a book like this can be very difficult if you don't manage the process. What does the final book look like? How many pages does it have? How many chapters? It is almost impossible to know in advance what the final product will look like. But, you must have some criteria in order to know when you're finished.

Many people don't write books or paint pictures because they feel that they won't know when they have a finished product. Others begin to write a book or paint a picture but since they never know when they're finished, they continuously improve it. They might eventually discard their work because they can't identify the finished product. You should always have some way of determining when you're finished or success will elude you.

You need to define what success looks like and realize how you'll recognize it when you achieve it. For example, I heard two men talking one day about success. One man was stressed because he came up short of his definition of success. The other man was content and relaxed because he had met his definition of success. I asked them what their definitions were. The man who was stressed was financially successful by our society's standards. However, he defined success as earning more than $1,000,000 a year, and he was a little bit short of that goal. The other man was much less financially successful, but he had defined success as waking up above ground (i.e. still alive). He felt successful every morning before he even got out of bed, and anything he achieved beyond that for the rest of the day was icing on the cake.

You should define your goal as something that is achievable. It should make you stretch in the direction in which you want to go to achieve a greater long term goal. You must not set a goal that is too low because then you'll never realize your true potential. At the same time, you must not set a goal that is unachievable because you'll get frustrated and give up. The two men in the previous example set goals that didn't inspire them. They both failed to set appropriate goals, one too high a goal and one too low a goal.

The *Rocks to Diamonds Cycle* has discrete steps as you go through each loop, so you should remember to create steps toward your goals. Each step should be achievable to build confidence and spur you on toward greater success. For example, if you want to learn something like sailing, you don't set a goal of being a captain after the first time out, even though being a captain is your long-term goal. Along the way, you set a goal of learning how to trim the sails. Then you set a higher goal of learning the points of sail. You keep raising the bar. By using this step method, you grow into our vision.

PERSISTENCE AND PERSEVERANCE

Dripping water hollows out stone,
Not through force;
But through persistence
—Ovid

One of the greatest determining factors of success is persistence or perseverance. Many people quit close to reaching their goals because they lose heart, stop believing, and give up. The person who has her heart set on a vision and won't give up until she achieves it will almost always be successful. The person who quits is by definition not successful.

You often hear of a singer or musician who is an "overnight success." People envy them because they seem to have gone from nothing to being hugely successful in what seems like a short period of time. But if you looked at the performers' past, you would find years and years of grinding it out, practicing, playing for unappreciative audiences, and not giving up their dream.

RESULT = BENEFIT OF OUR EFFORT

I grew up in Nova Scotia, in eastern Canada. It seemed like every time I went to a special event, the same girl was always singing. She often was unappreciated by her audience since she wasn't the headliner, but that never seemed to phase her. She just kept on singing and performing. Today that girl, Anne Murray, is a hugely successful international singer. To me, she exemplifies how perseverance is rewarded by success. She has been a great inspiration to me because she set such a great example of what a person could achieve through being persistent.

That is not to say that perseverance is always appropriate. Sometimes you have to look at the results of your intermediate steps and ask yourself if you are going in the right direction. A lack of success can be an indication that you're going down the wrong road. An example might be baseball players who focus solely on becoming professionals and then end up wasting many good years in dead-end attempts to get to the major leagues. There's a big difference between quitting your goals and modifying them based upon new information.

You must also balance what you're chasing with the cost of achieving it. As a youth I dreamed of being a politician and making a social contribution. However, I worked for a man who was a politician and saw the price he paid in his family life. After carefully assessing the pros and cons, I decided not to pursue that dream. The price was just too high for me. As it turned out, my choice allowed me to get into the absolutely right career, as a professor teaching accounting and computers.

WHERE DO YOU WANT TO GO FROM HERE?

You should always have a next goal. You should never have a final goal. When you achieve a goal, no matter how big, you always want to have a next goal to work towards. Do you want to continue to reach higher in the same direction? Do you want to change direction? Seldom does someone start on a long journey and complete it without changing course along the way.

When I was a young man, I saw that education was the way out of the dysfunctional home in which I had been raised. I went to university with the idea of becoming an engineer, but physics ended my engineering career in my first year. Then I took mathematics and chemistry and got my degree in those two subjects. Those subjects still didn't take me to where I wanted to go. But by getting my degree, I was moving in the right direction, as it opened the door for the next much more important step in my career. I went back to school and earned my Chartered Accountancy designation in Canada, and this got me a long way toward where I wanted to go. Later I got an MBA and Certified Public

Accountant certification in California, which further helped me along.

My overriding vision was that I would be a teacher. Where? When? Of what? I didn't know when I set out, but each of these steps got me closer to my ultimate goal. How could I tell if I achieved my goal? When I became a professor, I knew that I was doing what God had designed me to do. I never considered taking another job or even the same job at another university. Since I felt like California State University in Hayward was exactly where I was supposed to be, I stayed there for twenty-five years even though I had originally planned to stay for just one.

Life will have twists and turns that you won't be able to foresee, but if you keep a vision (even a blurry one) of success in your mind all the time, you will eventually get to the right place. More people who have a vision for their life succeed than those who don't have a vision or a plan or goals of any kind.

PATIENCE

One great weakness I see today is a lack of patience. It seems that too often people expect to get what they want right now. But one of the reasons victory can be so sweet is that it takes time to achieve. Just think of how great it is to graduate from university after years of hard work and sacrifice.

Think about the thrill of winning the World Series after a season of over two hundred games and years of conditioning and practice. Waiting patiently and working toward a goal make success all the more precious when you finally get it.

I feel that the lack of patience in personal financial matters is what has gotten our economy into the huge financial crisis that it is experiencing. I am afraid that people are missing the real lesson to be learned here because everyone is too busy blaming Wall Street and greed for the problem. The problem is a personal problem that individuals have created. While they blame others, they should accept their share of the responsibility.

Up to the 1960's banks offered very little credit, and it was difficult to obtain. Just think of a world with no credit cards or lines of credit. Believe it or not, people actually used cash! Even housing mortgages were much different than today. Generally they were smaller, shorter and harder to obtain. Bankers were some of the most conservative people in our society.

If you wanted something, you saved up your money until you could pay cash for it. Under these circumstances, people tended to make wiser decisions. One time a friend asked my advice about purchasing a car. She wondered what she should buy. I asked her how much money she had saved up for a car, and she said she had $5,000. I told her to buy a

$5,000 car. She ignored my advice and bought the car she wanted instead of the car she could afford.

Let's say you want to buy a car but no credit is available. You might save for two years and finally have $5,000. During those two years, you would most likely have been dreaming about getting your car. You would have been researching and test-driving the various cars that you could purchase. You would probably take lots of time to shop around to get the best car for $5,000. Once you purchased it, you would be extremely happy because you worked toward this goal for more than two years and made a financially sound decision.

However, this is not the way it is done today. Now someone starts by shopping for cars until they find the one they like, not the one they can afford or that fits their needs. Then they buy it using borrowed money. The more expensive the car, the greater the depreciation and the greater the interest they'll have to pay on the loan. Let me repeat that because this is double trouble that few people see when purchasing a vehicle.

When you purchase an expensive car, you have more depreciation (the loss in value of the car over time) and you have more interest (the cost of using someone else's money). The cost of insurance and sales taxes on an expensive car are also dramatically higher than on a less expensive car.

The thing that people fail to see here is that if they had purchased a $5,000 car with their savings, they'd have *no* monthly payments to make. They'd be free to spend or save their paychecks as they please. However, if they buy a car with borrowed money, they must repay that money with interest. This means that they've spent part of their subsequent paychecks before they've even earned them. *When you buy on credit, you give away part of your future.*

> When you buy on credit,
> you give away part of your future

Living a debt-free life is incredible. It may mean not having new cars or fancy toys, but it means having true freedom. When you get paid, you can do what you want with your money. There are many other benefits to debt-free living:

- no commitment to a bank
- better sleep
- lack of worry about making future payments
- fewer arguments with your spouse or partner.

One of the most common arguments couples have is about money. One of the primary reasons for divorce is debt. Young couples get into more debt than they can handle. The pressure on both of them is hard to deal with so they start arguing about it. Debt-free living eliminates this stress.

RESULT = BENEFIT OF OUR EFFORT

Debt-free living is possible for anyone if they will just lower their expectations and be patient.

There are a lot of benefits to patience and a lot of drawbacks to impatience. When going after a goal, you need to be patient with yourself and with the process but never stop pursuing it. Any goal that you hold for a long time and work diligently toward is more likely to be the right goal for you. You will appreciate it all the more once you achieve it.

If you're patient, you're more likely to be chasing the right goal because you have time to evaluate your goal along the way. Many people who buy cars on credit regret it later because they didn't take the time to consider what was right for them and work toward the goal of purchasing the right vehicle. Fewer people who save up regret their purchases because as they saved, they had time to assess their choice and research their options.

I believe that patience is a great virtue, and the practice of patience will increase the quality of your life and happiness immensely.

You must work toward your goals, and when you do not achieve them, you must not be disheartened. You must continue to learn from your past and improve your future. Do you need to modify your goal or continue to pursue it?

Eventually you will reach your chosen goal. It is a wonderful day when you have reached a long sought-after goal.

PERSONAL GROWTH EXERCISE:

Successful people can be divided into two groups:

1. Process-oriented people who care more about the process than the result. If such a person were to play tennis, he would enjoy the act of playing and not focus on the score at the end.

2. Results-oriented people who live for the result and don't care that much about the process. This type of person would focus on the score of a tennis match and who won rather than who played best or who had the most fun.

It is important to know your style when you make major decisions. For example, I am a results oriented person and when I am shopping, I don't enjoy the process and I get frustrated if it takes too long. A process oriented person might enjoy the time of looking and seeing all the different choices available. There is no right or wrong answer just. This is just an exercise to help you understand yourself better when going through the *Rocks to Diamond Cycle*.

RESULT = BENEFIT OF OUR EFFORT

Which kind of person are you?

_____
_____
_____

How does your style benefit you?

_____
_____
_____

How does your style hurt you?

_____
_____
_____

> **PLEASE, STOP AND COMPLETE THIS WRITTEN EXERCISE BEFORE GOING ON!**
>
> **BE PART OF THE SUCCESSFUL 2 PERCENT AND COMPLETE THE EXERCISE NOW!**

SUMMARY

Your efforts will get you closer to your stated goals. Keeping your long-term vision in mind will help you work toward short-term goals, as they are simply steps along the way toward the long-term vision for your life.

Two personal characteristics that will help you achieve goals are persistence and patience. If you do not possess these traits, you can develop them. They will keep you focused on your goals and keep you going when you seem to make little progress or encounter setbacks. Remember the saying of that great football coach Vince Lombardi, "*Winners never quit and quitters never win.*"

You need to be diligent in setting long term goals. As you work toward your short term goals you must always keep in mind your long term goals. This will mean that you will always have a goal to aim at and not suffer let down after you have achieved a goal.

Chapter Thirteen

BELIEF = CHANGED BY RESULT

*Your beliefs become your thoughts,
Your thoughts become your words,
Your words become your actions,
Your actions become your habits,
Your habits become your values,
Your values become your destiny.*
— Mahatma Gandhi

Each time you have progressed through the *Rocks to Diamonds Cycle,* your belief about yourself should have changed. Success breeds success while failure breeds failure. You learn from your past experiences and apply that knowledge to the future. People sometimes do that incorrectly. By that I mean that failing at something does not make you a failure. Failing means you simply didn't use the right methods to achieve success.

Then change methods and try, try again.

FEEDBACK LOOP

Every good system has a feedback loop that links the end of the process back to the beginning. For example, look at manufacturing cars. There is an inspection team at the end that tests the cars. They must communicate the findings to the people building the cars so the builders can improve the quality of the cars they build in the future. If there is no feedback then the quality will remain the same.

In the *Rocks to Diamonds Cycle*, the feedback connection is critical for believing in you. If you complete the first loop successfully, you have increased confidence going into the second loop. However, if you were unsuccessful at the end of the first loop, you'll have decreased confidence and have a harder time being successful in the second loop.

In my life, the first time the results part of the feedback loop were significant was in junior high school. Depending upon how students did in grade seven, they were grouped going into grade eight. I did well in grade seven (this is hard for me to believe, but apparently it was so). The next year, I went into grade 8A—the class with all the smart kids. Other students went into 8B, 8C, 8D, 8E, 8F, or 8G. Each subsequent letter indicated that you were a little lower on the academic food chain.

BELIEF = CHANGED BY RESULT

Even though we never knew it, grade seven (unlike any previous grade) decided our fate for the remainder of junior high school and high school. We were labeled and set on a path. Getting put into grade 8A was a great benefit for me. It has made a huge difference in my life. It is amazing that an educator's decision for a thirteen-year-old boy could so significantly set the path for his future.

I never doubted that I could achieve academically, even though my attitude almost sank my boat when I got into high school. During my elementary school years, my teachers saw me as someone who had great potential. I didn't see that and always hated their comments on my report cards that I was not working to my potential. However, that stayed with me and gave me some confidence during my troubled years in high school.

Today, I realize that their reinforcement of the idea that I had great potential got inside me and gave me confidence to go to university and later to undertake my accounting studies. The fact that I was chosen to go to grade 8A was a huge boost to my self-confidence that lasted throughout my life.

Constant feedback from my teachers helped me to see myself in a different light. Although on the surface I continued to act with a bad attitude, internally I must have accepted their comments and retained them. Today I can see that they were correct in their assessment but it didn't come to fruition until late in life.

MEASURING BELIEF IN YOURSELF

It would be great if there was a device like a bathroom scale that could measure self-confidence. You could measure how much you believed in yourself at various times along the way to your goal to see if you were improving in self-confidence. That would also help you determine if you needed to work on your self-confidence in some way.

I know one of the greatest confidence boosts I ever received came completely out of the blue. When I had become an accountant, I dreamed of being a teacher but had low self-confidence. Without self-confidence, I was unable to talk in front of a group of people. This was a major hindrance for a teacher.

Then a man named Ross Towler, a leader in the accounting community in my hometown, contacted me and asked if I would be interested in taking a course at Toastmasters. He explained that it was an organization that helps people become better speakers. The special course called *Speechcraft* met one night a week for the next eight weeks.

The first three weeks, I didn't say one word to anyone. Not only did I lack self-confidence, but I discovered that because of my low self-esteem I was terrified of getting up in front of people and talking.

The Toastmasters were patient and encouraging, and the third week, at the very end of the meeting I stood up and said something for the first time. In the eighth week, I was the chairman of the meeting. I had discovered a hidden talent that no one knew was inside of me. Especially me! After that, public speaking became one of my favorite things to do. There are few things in my life that compare to the thrill of talking to a group of people and teaching them something that will improve their lives.

This continues today. After I retired from teaching I went back to Toastmasters and am having a ton of fun speaking and learning and teaching in Toastmasters.

You never know when some event will happen to increase or decrease your self-confidence. It is important to try to monitor your self-confidence and to build it up in whatever way you can. You can build self-confidence by getting an education, by learning a new skill, by losing weight, by giving up a bad habit, or by excelling in a hobby. The best way I know is to join Toastmasters and learn to speak in public. The speaking will lead to a huge boost in your self-confidence. *Self-confidence comes from success, whether it is big or small, in any area of life.*

Self-confidence comes from success, whether it is big or small, in any area of life

Do you have self-confidence or self-consciousness? Self-confidence will improve your performance in every aspect of life. Self-consciousness will hamper your performance and will often prevent you from trying something that could be wonderful. A friend recently expressed this in a different manner. He said that upon entering a room full of people, what do you think? Do you think, "Here I am, I hope someone likes me." (self-consciousness) or, "Here I am, I hope to meet some interesting people." (self-confidence).

CHANGE BELIEF TO CERTAINTY

The greater your self-confidence when beginning something new, the better is your chance of success. But just think if you could raise your confidence to certainty.

Let's look at golf. Many people who play golf lack self-confidence in their skills. Each time they play, they remember all the bad shots they've taken. This can turn what belief they had in themselves to absolute certainty that they're bad at golf. Guess how they play!

On a typical day of golfing a player may have 80% poor shots and 20% good shots (remember the 80/20 rule?). It is important that he forget the bad shots and remember only the good shots. By remembering only the good shots that he made, he would realize that he has the skills to make any shot.

Golf consists of three types of shots: long shots, short shots, and putts. On any given day, a player will make a few good shots of each of these types. Those good shots may not be the majority, but that doesn't matter. Even a few is enough to show him that he has the skill to make any shot. Once he believes that he can make a shot, he just needs to focus on doing it.

Whatever your field of endeavor, you must build your self-confidence. If you strengthen your belief in you until that belief becomes a certainty, you will be much more successful. Building self-confidence in one aspect of your life will improve your self-confidence in other areas of your life.

A funny thing about confidence is that it spills over into other areas of your life. If you become confident in one area, you will become more confident overall. The self-confidence a person exudes opens a lot of doors in his or her life. Strong self-confidence attracts people to you while weak self-confidence will push people away. In dating I see that strong self-confidence will attract good people. However, weak self-confidence often attracts the wrong kind of people.

There is a saying that "*The rich get richer and the poor get poorer.*" That really applies to self-confidence. You could say that the people with strong self-confidence get stronger while the people with weak self-confidence get weaker. So you need to work at building up your self-confidence. If you do, you'll see a big improvement in all areas.

I don't know of anything that will make a bigger difference in your life than improving your self-confidence. Since it is so critical to every aspect of your life including your relationship with yourself, I can't say enough about working on your self-confidence.

Finally, self-confidence is a very healthy characteristic to possess. It is not arrogance. Strong self-confidence is thinking highly of yourself which you should. Arrogance is thinking too highly of yourself and too lowly of other people. Arrogance is a symptom of low self-esteem and insecurity.

CHANGING YOUR BELIEF

When you approach something new, your attitude will often determine the outcome. If you approach something believing that you can master it, then you can. But, if you start by believing that you can't master this new thing, then you won't.

When I taught introductory accounting, it was a required course for all students majoring in business. Many students would enter the class with a terrible attitude that could lead to disaster. It was not unusual to hear a student say:

BELIEF = CHANGED BY RESULT

"My friend took this accounting course last year and said that it was the hardest course ever."

Or my personal favorite:

"I heard that this course is really difficult, so I'll take it this fall and fail and then I'll retake it in the winter and pass."

Usually they got the first part of this belief correct. How could they succeed when they began with this attitude?

I spent time the first day of class each quarter trying to change this belief. I heard the same things when I first started to study accounting, but that just motivated me to study harder. I found the tests weren't so difficult, and my grades reflected my hard work. Grades reflect belief; either you believe that you can do it or you believe that you can't do it. It really doesn't matter how easy or difficult the material is.

Students in my classes were required to do lots of homework. An important aspect of learning accounting is doing the homework. This not only helps them learn the material, but it also builds confidence in their ability to do the work. This is an example of the *Rocks to Diamonds Cycle*. Every time a student did a homework problem, they either increased or decreased their belief about being able to do accounting.

I tried to make all my tests and exams a fair reflection of what I taught in class. To measure each class's performance, I used statistics and expected to see a bell curve, with most grades concentrated around a certain point. For example, if the median grade was 70 percent, I'd expect to find lots of students with scores between 60 and 80 percent and fewer students with grades in the 50s and in the 80s and even fewer below 50 or over 90.

But, in accounting classes, the grades typically formed two bell curves instead of one. One bell curve was centered on 75 percent and the other on 40 percent. What caused the difference? It was simply the amount of effort the students put into the course. One group studied and did their homework while the other group didn't.

What many students also discovered was that when they applied themselves to the material in the accounting course, it wasn't as hard as they had imagined. When they did the assigned homework problems, they found they weren't as hard as the students thought they'd be. Each homework problem that they completed successfully raised their level of belief in themselves and their ability to do accounting. This was the *Rocks to Diamond Cycle* in action. Each time they completed a cycle, their self-confidence rose higher. Some got to the point of certainty and earned A grades on exams, and some even went on to become accountants.

Did this success affect other parts of their lives? Since they could handle what they had perceived as one of the most difficult courses in their degree program, this increased their self-confidence in other courses and also in other areas of life. Success breeds more success because it increases your self-confidence.

You need to use this concept to your advantage in life. Whatever you do, you should work hard and do your best at it. Afterward, you should be aware of how well you did and let that bolster your self-confidence. Then you can take on bigger challenges. You can take on tasks that you thought were too difficult just to prove to yourself that you can do them. Who knows, you may find your purpose in the process.

CHALLENGE YOURSELF

> *Accept the Challenges So That You May Feel the Exhilaration of Victory*
> **—General George Patton**

When I was younger, I did not have the courage to try new things. I played it safe by only doing what I knew I could achieve. If I tried something new, I had low expectations of what I could do and settled for poor results. I wasn't competitive because I had little self-confidence.

I always loved hiking for many reasons such as being outdoors, smelling the fresh air, getting exercise and seeing God's wonderful creation. But also for me, it was a noncompetitive activity. I could hike as well as or better than my friends because I have long legs and great stamina. Therefore, hiking was a nonthreatening activity. Plus no one kept score like in sports.

When I was in my thirties went on a weekend backpacking trip that changed my life. I signed up with a hiking group expecting some hiking and overnight camping. This trip took place over Easter weekend, so it lasted three days and two nights. The group was to go from Sunol to Del Valle in the San Francisco East Bay.

The trip started in the morning on Good Friday from Sunol and the group hiked to a camping area for the first night. The hike was nothing unusual. We camped out on a cliff overlooking a large canyon. In the middle of the night, I got up and was overcome by the beauty. I can still picture it today as clear as a bell. When I first got out of my tent, I was struck by the bright full moon. I have never seen the moon bigger or brighter than it was that night. I felt like it was closer than normal. Then I walked to the edge of the cliff and was literally overwhelmed with the sight of the canyon.

When I moved to San Francisco, the fog really amazed me. I grew up in a foggy place, and the fog was just there. But in San Francisco, the fog is different; it flows like water in slow motion. I love to watch it flow over a hill or around the city or past the Golden Gate Bridge on its way into the bay.

On this night, the fog flowed into the canyon below and almost filled it. It looked like the canyon was full of white cotton batting. I wanted to jump on top of it and play in it. The full moon shining on the canyon filled with fog was one of the most beautiful sights I have ever seen. It seemed to glow in the moonlight. I didn't attend church at that time, but I didn't doubt that there was a God. How else could there be such beauty in the world?

That evening was just the beginning of the miracles of that weekend. The next day we hiked up and down mountains like there was no end to them. I can remember hiking up one mountain and thinking how difficult it was. I thought that I saw the top just ahead. When I got there, I learned that it wasn't the top but it was just a curve in the trail. This happened over and over until finally I said to myself:

"There is no top, only more curves in the trail."

Basically I had given up hope of finding the top of the mountain.

That was the second great thing that happened that weekend. I not only learned how to think about hiking in the mountains but also about living life. What I learned was that as I work toward a goal, it may not be just around the next curve but instead is somewhere off in the distance. If I keep that distant goal in mind, each curve is just another step closer to the goal. Instead of hiking on an emotional roller coaster, experiencing a high when I expected the top and a low when I discovered it wasn't there, I learned that each segment was just part of the journey. I learned to just enjoy that leg of the journey and then the next leg and the next.

After that weekend I thought about the hike and the fact that I went more than twenty miles while carrying a heavy backpack up and down mountains. If I had known that beforehand, I wouldn't have gone on the trip. But when I looked back on it, what I had thought impossible was only difficult and could be accomplished when it was broken down into small segments. I always knew I could do the next leg. If that mountain trail had gone straight to the top instead of curving, I would have quit and believed I couldn't do it.

So it is with life. The path to a goal may seem long and impossible, but when you break it down into small pieces, it is easier to achieve. For example, getting a university degree may sound tough, but when you look at it one semester or one course at a time, it appears doable.

The month after the backpacking trip, I was amazed at what I had accomplished. I started to look for other challenges, not competing against other people, but simply trying to find out what I could do. What else could I accomplish that I thought was impossible for me to do?

I found my next one in riding my bicycle. Riding my bike was always a favorite hobby, but true to my nature, I didn't go on any rides that were too difficult. I lived near Mt. Diablo, which rises to a height of 3,849 feet above sea level and has a lookout on top. The road up was 11 miles long with lots of curves, just like the hike. The elevation gain was over 3,000 feet, which I felt was clearly impossible for a guy like me.

I decided that riding to the lookout on Mt. Diablo was my next challenge. I took my bike to the bottom of the mountain. My goal for the day was to ride to the first gate about three miles up. Then each day I would ride farther until I reached the top. The ride to the first gate wasn't as difficult as I had thought and was actually a lot of fun. Instead of feeling tired when I got there, I felt excited and energized. So I pushed on to the next milestone, which was at six miles. That section was less steep than the first, so it also was not as hard as I had thought.

Now I was more than halfway up the mountain and still feeling good. I started the third leg, which was a lot steeper, and after about a mile, I was dead tired. But I was feeling elated because I had done more than I thought possible for me. I didn't make it to the top that day, but I did many times after that, and I felt like a winner every time. Not only was I seeing the mountain's beauty and doing something that few people living in the area do, I was challenging myself and surprising myself by accomplishing more than I thought I could.

After this I looked at my fears and insecurities and wondered about I would like to tackle. The next challenge I undertook was acting in a play. I had been a professor for a few years and found it enjoyable. Acting in a play seemed a whole lot scarier. In the next two years, I acted in two plays and enjoyed them a great deal. Once again, I surprised myself by doing something that I thought was impossible for me.

You must believe in yourself. Before the hiking trip on Easter weekend, my belief in myself was limited. I believed I could only do the easy things in life. However, completing that hike taught me that I could also do difficult things in life. Riding up the mountain and acting in the plays verified that idea.

I also saw that not only had my belief in myself changed, but my belief itself had also changed, to certainty. I went from believing I could only do the easy things to believing that I could also do the difficult things and then to knowing with certainty that I could accomplish anything I set out to do. Writing this book has been my latest challenge, and I approached it without any doubt of accomplishing it.

The other lesson in all of this is that belief in yourself carries over to other aspects of your life. If you have a poor belief about yourself, then you will have poor self-confidence and self-esteem, and it will affect other areas of life. However, if you have a strong belief in yourself, then you will have strong self-confidence, which will spill over into all aspects of life.

Belief in yourself, or self-confidence, is critical to living life successfully. I see many people with so much potential inside but who are afraid to try anything because they lack self-confidence. I want to really encourage you to try new things, to challenge yourself and go into the challenge believing you can do it. Just watch what happens.

Here is another aspect of self-confidence that you may appreciate. Many people find self-confidence attractive. When a person walks into a room they give off signals of their level of self-confidence. Other people in the room pick up on those signals and respond appropriately. For years I gave off signals of low self-confidence and when I entered a room I felt insecure and people responded by avoiding me. Now I walk into a room with a big smile and an open demeanor and people respond by being very open and friendly.

PERSONAL GROWTH EXERCISE:

Make a list of challenges that you would like to undertake. Start by simply writing down every idea you think of without evaluating it. Once you're finished, look the list over and evaluate them, then determine timelines for undertaking them. For example, pick one that you would like to do this coming month, pick a few for the next year, others for the next five years, and leave some as long term with no set time to tackle them.

_____

_____

_____

_____

_____

_____

_____

_____

_____

_____

_____

_____

Once you're ready to undertake a challenge, turn it into a written goal and focus on it. It will happen!

> **PLEASE, STOP AND COMPLETE THIS WRITTEN EXERCISE BEFORE GOING ON!**
>
> **BE PART OF THE SUCCESSFUL 2 PERCENT AND COMPLETE THE EXERCISE NOW!**

SUMMARY

Belief in yourself is critical to success in any area of your life. You need to evaluate how strong or weak your self-confidence is at a particular moment. Then you need to work toward improving your self-confidence by finding challenges and then completing them successfully. This will raise your self-image and make future challenges easier to achieve.

It is one thing to hope or believe that you can achieve something, it is much better to be certain that you can do it. You need to raise the level of belief in yourself to certainty. Just think how easy something would be if you were certain that you could do it before you even started.

Once you have improved your self-confidence, you can start to challenge yourself in different areas. You can try new things that you might have found to be intimidating previously. I find it unbelievable what I can achieve today compared to before I started my personal growth.

Section Four:

CHANGING YOUR LIFE

Chapter Fourteen

YES YOU CAN!

> *Everyone thinks of changing the world,
> But no one thinks of changing himself.*
> **—Leo Tolstoy**

I truly believe that you are capable of doing great things in your lifetime. I know that I have accomplished way more than I ever thought possible when I was in high school or even in my twenties and thirties.

Life is a challenge that we can face head on and enjoy or shrink away from and merely exist instead of truly living.

I hope that at this point in the book you are motivated to live your life in a fuller way to achieve the happiness and success that you deserve. It will never be given to you but it is there for you to take whenever you are ready.

ACTION IS CRITICAL

One of the difficulties about writing a self-help book is not knowing what you, the reader, will get out of it. The reason I put exercises in the book is so you'll *do* activities and learn the lessons better. That will make the book's points more meaningful. I firmly believe that only by action can you achieve your goals and succeed.

I learned this in high school chemistry. One day our teacher told us that sodium was very reactive with water. Those of us who were listening heard this fact and some even wrote it down, but no one knew what it really meant. About a month later during chemistry laboratory, the teacher took a small piece of sodium and placed it in a petri dish. Then he put some water on it. At first we weren't that interested since we had all seen something get wet before. However, we were astonished when instead of getting wet, the sodium burst into flames in a very violent reaction. It was completely consumed within a matter of seconds. Seeing that reaction was critical to understanding what the teacher meant.

Just as we needed to see that reaction to understand the teacher's lesson, only by doing can you accomplish. You can read a million self-help and motivational books, but they won't benefit you one bit unless you do what the authors recommend. You will never know how much you can change until you have *done* something yourself.

YOU CAN ACHIEVE ANYTHING

You can do anything, but not everything
—David Allen

I have found this chapter the hardest to write because it is the least definite. The previous chapters were about things that I have experienced and lived personally, but this chapter is about the limitless possibilities that exist in your life and not what I have experienced in my life. You truly have no limits except those you put on yourself.

When I say, *"you will never know how much you can change yourself"*, I mean that no matter what you achieve in life, there will always be the possibility of achieving more. I'm not suggesting that you should always be chasing more, but possibilities are always there if you want them. Often a person accomplishes less in life than possible because he limits himself. He becomes his own worst enemy.

Many people I know think of winning the lottery or retirement as the end. I hear things like, "I'm going to play golf every day," or "I'm going to go fishing every day." These people don't do well in retirement or after winning the lottery. If their only reason to get out of bed in the morning is to do the same thing that they've done for the past year, they'll end up staying in bed. People need to have a purpose in life or they'll become unhappy and unmotivated to do anything. This applies to everyone.

If you won $10 million in the lottery, what would you do? It's nice to dream, but reality is usually much different. Personally, I think winning the lottery would be a great burden. Life would become focused on the money—how to protect it, how to minimize income taxes, how to invest it, how to spend it, and so on. I know when we think of that prize now, it sounds great. However, after the euphoria wears off and reality sets in, life would be different in many ways, some good and some bad.

> *You will never know how much you can change yourself*

I don't buy lottery tickets because I'm afraid that I might win and that would probably change my life for the worse. If I did win $10 million, I think I would find 10 friends, churches, and charitable organizations and give each one $1 million.

But let's return to the question. If you won $10 million, what would you do? Let's look down the road five years. What do you do each day? How do you spend your time? Is your life full of meaning? If it is, you are unusual. Almost every story I have read about people who won a lottery was a story of a ruined life. Often their lives were so empty a few years after they won that they turned to drugs and alcohol. It is said that the money won't change you; it will just magnify who you already are. It seems to find your weakness and make that your main characteristic.

It doesn't matter where you are in life today; you can change yourself in the present moment (remember that the present is the only time in which you have that power) so that your future is better. If you do this every day, then every following day will be better. You don't need to progress with giant steps. Baby steps work just fine. But the key is consistent improvement.

When I was studying to become an accountant and my classmates completed their exams after three long hard years of work and study, many fell into the trap of letdown. They had worked hard and been so focused on this great goal that they failed to set a subsequent goal. Since they didn't have another goal to strive toward, some fell into the trap of just doing what was in their lives. For an accountant, there is always an endless amount of work, so they ended up working a lot of extra time and not creating new goals.

Since I had teaching as my long-term goal, becoming an accountant was just a milestone along the way. My friend

Dave wanted to be a lawyer, so becoming an accountant was just a milestone along the path he had chosen. But those who had no subsequent goal often got lost in their work.

Individuals who achieve great things or have very successful lives have goals for five years, ten years, and twenty years ahead. They frequently update them so that when they accomplish one goal, they have the next to strive toward. Next goals don't have to be a continuation of previous goals. They might be in a different area of life, such as a relationship goal, a health goal, or a personal growth goal.

It is not unusual for people to progress through education goals, then career goals, relationship goals, family goals, and so on. No matter what your focus is, you should always have some career goals because in today's world, if you're not growing in your career, you will be falling behind. Even when relationship and family goals become a bigger part of your life, you need to maintain career goals such as learning new software, taking a course to enhance your skills, or learning whatever is appropriate for your career.

By always having future goals planned out, you will always be focused on where you are going. You are guaranteed to get a lot further in life if you know where it is you're headed.

KNOW YOUR BIG PICTURE

> *You must find a cause to believe in*
> *Or spend the rest of your life*
> *Compensating yourself for failure*
> **—John Powell**

It always amused me that when I counseled students and asked them what the big picture of their lives was, many either didn't know or hadn't thought about it. The only goal they possessed was finishing the degree that they were currently undertaking. There was a giant void after that.

I encouraged them to start thinking of the big picture of their lives. It is not a specific goal or set of goals but simply what they saw for their life in general terms. My big picture was to be a teacher. I didn't know the details beyond that image.

I was successful in my career because I was fortunate to have had good direction early in life. However, it wasn't until my twenties that I figured things out. A career in accounting suited my gifts well. A career in teaching meant discovering and developing more gifts and talents that I was blessed with.

I am happy with my life and feel successful because I did and still am doing what I was designed to do.

No matter what your age, you should have a big picture for the remainder of your life. If your big picture is what you currently have, then you have stopped growing and have started dying - not a happy idea.

In order to clarify and develop your big picture, let's do an exercise. If you are twenty or thirty years old, this exercise will be much different than if you are sixty or seventy years old. A big picture of a future of fifty or sixty years is much different than the big picture of preparing your bucket list. However, a big picture is critical at any age.

PERSONAL GROWTH EXERCISE:

Describe the big picture that you currently see for your life. Try to include as many areas of your life as possible and don't just focus on your career. What do you see happening in the areas of family, relationships, health, career, finances, hobbies, challenges? Remember that this is not a lot of specific goals as much as a general, broad description of what you want or expect for your future.

_____
_____
_____
_____
_____

Another related exercise can help you see your big picture. List one hundred things that you want to do before you die. Whether you're twenty or eighty, you can make this list by simply writing down (without evaluation or judgment of any kind) things that you would like to do assuming you're able to do them.

Use the Magic Wand principal. Assume that you have a magic wand. Whatever you want you just have to wave your magic wand and it will magically appear.

(Many people find it hard to come up with 100. Keep plugging away because the more you do, the more you get in touch with what you really want.)

You may find it difficult to complete a list of one hundred items. Keep going because once you run out of ideas, you will probably start getting to the really good ones that you haven't let yourself dream about but that may be your real big picture.

1. _____
2. _____
3. _____
4. _____
5. _____

6. _____
7. _____
8. _____
9. _____
10. _____
11. _____
12. _____
13. _____
14. _____
15. _____
16. _____
17. _____
18. _____
19. _____
20. _____
21. _____
22. _____
23. _____
24. _____
25. _____
26. _____

27. _____
28. _____
29. _____
30. _____
31. _____
32. _____
33. _____
34. _____
35. _____
36. _____
37. _____
38. _____
39. _____
40. _____
41. _____
42. _____
43. _____
44. _____
45. _____
46. _____
47. _____

48. _____
49. _____
50. _____
51. _____
52. _____
53. _____
54. _____
55. _____
56. _____
57. _____
58. _____
59. _____
60. _____
61. _____
62. _____
63. _____
64. _____
65. _____
66. _____
67. _____
68. _____

69. _____
70. _____
71. _____
72. _____
73. _____
74. _____
75. _____
76. _____
77. _____
78. _____
79. _____
80. _____
81. _____
82. _____
83. _____
84. _____
85. _____
86. _____
87. _____
88. _____
89. _____

90. _____
91. _____
92. _____
93. _____
94. _____
95. _____
96. _____
97. _____
98. _____
99. _____
100. _____

> **PLEASE, STOP AND COMPLETE THIS WRITTEN EXERCISE BEFORE GOING ON!**
>
> **BE PART OF THE SUCCESSFUL 2 PERCENT AND COMPLETE THE EXERCISE NOW!**

DECIDE WHAT YOU MUST GIVE

The more clearly you've described your big picture and set goals to match it, the easier it will be for you to see what you'll need to give to get what you want. I had to give years of studying, earning degrees, and working in accounting offices to become skilled enough to be an accounting professor. I never stopped studying, and I later became a professor in computing as well.

If you want to be a doctor, you'll need to study and practice medicine until you're a skilled physician. But the giving won't stop then, as you'll have to continue to learn to keep abreast of the advances in medicine.

Mark wanted to be a mechanic. He chose to study and spend time working on his trade to be a skilled mechanic. While many of his workmates stopped learning, he continued to take classes and soon rose above the others to become an outstanding mechanic. Mark gave what was required to rise above the rest.

To achieve anything, you'll need to give something of yourself. You'll have to learn skills and then continue to keep them up. The more successful you want to be, the more effort you will have to give to rise to the top and to stay at the top once you've arrived. There are no free rides in life. As

Zig Ziglar says, "*The elevator to success is closed but the stairs are always open.*"

The only jobs that you can get in life without giving of yourself are not jobs you would dream of having for a career. I call these "motivational jobs" because they motivate you to get an education or a better job. The same is true with anything in life: the things that come with little effort on your part are not usually what you want.

If you have set goals and are determined to achieve them, then you see the effort, or cost, as nothing compared to the benefit that you are going to receive. It is simply the cost-benefit analysis: you weigh the cost against the value of the benefit to see if something is worth pursuing.

However, if your goals are unclear or if you're not focused on them, then you might focus too much on the cost and be unwilling to pay the price. For example, if you are dedicated to being a doctor, then the years of preparation are a price that you are willing to pay. But if you are not *dedicated* to becoming a doctor and instead focus on the years of study and preparation as undesirable, then you will probably not be willing to pay the price to be a doctor.

I know I was so dedicated to being a professor that I never looked at the study as a cost or hardship but as a pleasure. I truly enjoyed my years of schooling and working in accounting firms as I got ready to teach. If you don't enjoy the time of preparation, then there is a strong possibility that you won't enjoy the end result either.

I saw a student who got straight A's in his classes and earned his accounting degree. When he became an accountant, he hated the work and quit after less than a year. When I asked him why, he said that he never enjoyed the study to get his degree. He had just done it because his father was an accountant. He was trying to please his father rather than living his own dreams.

When you learn a new skill for a hobby, you don't think of that work as undesirable but as part of the pleasure of the hobby. Striving toward any goal works the same way. The preparation is part of the process, and it should be as enjoyable as the goal that you have set for yourself.

You can learn more about paying the price for goals in the book, *What Price Are You Willing to Pay?* by John C. Maxwell. I feel that he presents the whole subject excellently.

Although I use terms like "cost" and "effort" when describing preparation, it really is nothing more than enjoying every part of what you have chosen to do. Remember, your attitude is everything in life. It will determine how you see things before you do them and also how you view them after they are completed.

ATTITUDE OF GRATITUDE

To Thine Own Self Be True.
—Polonius in Shakespeare's Hamlet

If you want to have the greatest success in any area of your life or you want to experience life with the greatest degree of fulfillment, then adopting an *"Attitude of Gratitude"* is important.

Attitude of Gratitude

I discovered this when I was just beginning therapy after getting divorced. I was bitter and angry because I felt that I had lost so much in the divorce. My therapist gave me a homework exercise to list the ten good things that I got from the marriage. I told him that I could easily give him a list of the ten things that I lost in the divorce but that he was crazy to think that I had gotten anything good out of it.

He told me that every situation has two sides. You need to look at the good side and the bad side in order to better understand what really happened. Once you've done that, you must forget the bad things and focus on the good things so that you can find peace. Focusing on the bad things will only lead to hurt, resentment, and anger, which in turn will lead to more problems in the future.

I went home from that session sure that I couldn't do the exercise, but since I trusted my therapist, I was determined to do the best I could do. At first I really struggled with the exercise. However, by the time the next meeting had arrived, not only had I done the exercise but I was a different person. I had made a list of the ten things that I had gotten out of the marriage. In addition, I realized that the things that I had received were of infinite value to me and the things that I had given up were insignificant. I don't mean valuable in terms of money but in terms of my set of values. After that, instead of being bitter and angry at what I had lost, I was happy and thankful for what I had gained.

The exercise that my therapist gave me is an incredible one. You can use it whenever you're struggling with a situation. First, you list the bad parts of the situation. This should be easy since you're usually already focused on them. (By the way, there is healing power in writing down the negatives and then later filing or throwing them away). Second, you make a list of the good parts of the situation. Then you can forget the bad parts and focus on the good parts. This is truly an excellent way to get over a bad situation and find peace.

I know that it may look like there is nothing good about your situation. I have found that every situation has both positive and negative features. If you focus on the bad, it may break you. *If you focus on the good, it will grow you.* Adversity is a part of everyone's life. *It is not the adversity that determines who you are; it is your response to it that shows who you are.*

If you focus on the good, it will grow you

As an example, let's look at two people with similar skills who get laid off. One is bitter and angry and feels wronged by the layoff. He then starts feeling sorry for himself (which is very dangerous) because of what happened *to* him. This carries over into his job search, making it more difficult for him to get another job. By feeling sorry for himself, he may also turn to drugs and alcohol to numb his bad feelings. He has started to self-destruct.

The other individual is angry for a short time but then sees that this is an opportunity to get a new job. Maybe a job with a better company or a better boss! She is excited by the opportunity and goes out and enthusiastically pursues another job. She probably will get a better job and is unlikely to turn to drugs and alcohol because she doesn't need to numb her feelings.

Both people faced the same situation, but each had a very different response to it and a different outcome. Many people who run their own businesses started after getting laid off from a job. These people are often happier than they were in their jobs and look back at getting laid off with gratitude. They wouldn't be where they are today without having been forced to evaluate their lives and what they wanted to do.

PERSONAL GROWTH EXERCISE:

Whenever you are struggling with a situation try this exercise to put things in perspective. Make a list of 5 or 10 bad and then good parts of your situation. You're probably already focused on the bad ones so this should be fairly easy. Remember, there is healing power in writing down the negatives and then later filing or throwing them away.

First, make a list of 5 or 10 bad parts of the situation.

_____
_____
_____
_____
_____

Secondly, make a list of the good parts of the situation.

_____
_____
_____
_____
_____

> **PLEASE, STOP AND COMPLETE THIS WRITTEN EXERCISE BEFORE GOING ON!**
>
> **BE PART OF THE SUCCESSFUL 2 PERCENT AND COMPLETE THE EXERCISE NOW!**

In everything that you do in life, you need to adopt an *Attitude of Gratitude* and view every situation as a positive growing experience. One way I use my *Attitude of Gratitude* is by saying grace before every meal. No matter where I am or who I am with, I always stop before I eat and thank God for whatever is good in my life at that time. You can always find something good in your life if you just look for it.

An important part of adopting a positive attitude is resolving past hurts – everyone has them. This can be done through forgiveness. If you feel that someone has wronged you, you may live with negative feelings that if left unchecked, can lead to serious problems. However, if you can forgive that other person, you can get past these feelings. You will feel like a huge burden has been removed from your body.

Forgiveness is something that you do for you, not for the other person. After all, the person who wronged you may not even know how you feel and may be unable to receive your forgiveness. If you focus on yourself, forgiveness is easier. It is freeing. One approach to forgiveness is to think about the other person and ask yourself why he or she did something bad to you. You will probably realize that he or she acted out of inner pain and not from malicious intent. If you can't forgive, then you carry those feelings around through life like dragging an anchor behind you. But if you can forgive the person, you can move on with your life free of that burdensome anchor.

There is a saying that is very helpful in this area. I have found it to be true in so many cases:

"Hurt people hurt people."

> Hurt people
> hurt people

I'm not suggesting that forgiveness is easy, but it is very important for you to resolve these past issues. I know of no other way of changing from living in the past to living in the present and working toward your goals for the future. It is difficult to develop an *Attitude of Gratitude* if you haven't forgiven people in your past.

PERSONAL GROWTH EXERCISE:

Choose some incident from your past that gives you hurt feelings today. This could be a small or big event. This could be from yesterday or in your childhood. Anything that is negative and you are carrying it around will need to be eliminated from your life.

First, describe the event as best you remember it.

_____
_____
_____
_____

Secondly, describe why you think that other person did it.

_____
_____
_____
_____

Thirdly, write down a prayer for that other person. Pray that he might heal this problem within him so that not will he be free but he will stop hurting others. Also write down a prayer of thankfulness that you are free from the negative feelings that have been affecting your life. Pray this prayer every time the old bad feeling come up until they are gone away.

_____
_____
_____
_____

You can repeat this exercise for each wound that you have received from others. After a while you will have healed all your wounds and be more free to live your life. I can remember the exact time when my last would was healed. It felt like a giant hole inside of me closer grew smaller until one in therapy I felt to close completely. What a great day that was.

> **PLEASE, STOP AND COMPLETE THIS WRITTEN EXERCISE BEFORE GOING ON!**
>
> **BE PART OF THE SUCCESSFUL 2 PERCENT AND COMPLETE THE EXERCISE NOW!**

My friends have a little boy named Derek who I feel is a model for what it means to have an *Attitude of Gratitude*. One evening at dinner, Derek's mother asked him to say grace as he often did. The whole family bowed their heads, but there was complete silence. Finally, a little voice said, "God, I don't like what we are having for dinner tonight, but I want to thank you anyway."

That is the true *Attitude of Gratitude*. In every situation in life, whether in good or bad circumstances, you need to look for something to be thankful for. It will change how you experience your life, and you will be much happier because of it. You will also influence the people around you with your attitude, so you need to focus on having a wonderful attitude.

This *Attitude of Gratitude* can really change your life. Many people tend to focus on the negative more than the positive. When you talk with people, some only tell you what is wrong with their lives or the weather. These are seldom uplifting encounters. However, if you choose to share the good and ask others what's going well in their lives, then the focus switches and you'll have an uplifting exchange. The other person will walk away feeling a little better about their day also.

Ask yourself, what's good in your life today?

- ☑ Can you see?
- ☑ Can you hear?
- ☑ Can you walk?
- ☑ Do you live in a free country?
- ☑ Are you able to choose what you do today?
- ☑ Is there someone in your life who loves you?

All of these are good things that not everyone can enjoy. For each of these items that you possess, you have reason to be thankful.

SUMMARY

Action is critical to anything you want to accomplish in life. You can't just think it or wish for it or read about it, you must take action to accomplish it. The more that you do, the more you can do. Just like your physical muscles, your life will grow larger as you accomplish more. The more you give of yourself, the more results you will see.

Once you examine situations in your life, it is easy to come up with two lists, a list of bad things and a list of good things. You should forget the bad things and focus on the good things all day. You will find that the list will grow longer every day.

Forgiveness plays an important part in your getting over your past and living in the present. No matter what the situation, forgive and forget, and move on with life. It is easier said than done but it is critical for your emotional freedom.

In everything that you do, you should adopt an *Attitude of Gratitude* and fill your life with diamonds.

Chapter Fifteen

LET'S GO!

> *The secret to getting ahead*
> *Is getting started*
> **—Mark Twain**

It is time for you to take action on what you want to do. Hopefully you have done the exercises that I recommended and you are seeing changes in your life. If not, please, please, please get started. Obviously you can never make progress if you don't start. The number one difference between those who are successful and those who aren't is taking action.

Tomorrow is not early enough, today, right now is the time to start. Get up and get a piece of paper and outline some goals or plans and then take steps today and every day for the rest of your life towards achieving your goals.

I know that your life will be better once you start to grow.

I hope that you have enjoyed reading *Attitude Determines Destiny*. If you're excited to use this material but are unsure of where to start, this chapter will help.

I want to introduce a program I call GAS, which will energize your life in a short period of time. I believe that if you follow this program, you will see amazing changes within the next thirty days.

GAS is an acronym for:

GOALS + ACTION = SUCCESS

Here is a thirty-day challenge that will demonstrate the power of goals.

STEP 1 SET A GOAL

Pick one of your goals. The goal should not be too big but one that you really want to accomplish. Write it below:

_____

_____

_____

Write the goal on a three-by-five card and carry it with you for the next thirty days. Refer to it several times every day. Read it aloud as often as possible.

Write your goal on a piece of paper and make at least five copies and hang them up in your home, your car, and your work space so that you'll be reminded of your goal often. Think about the goal every time you see one of your signs.

Review your goal first thing every morning when you arise and last thing every night before you go to sleep.

These reminders will establish your goal firmly in your conscious and subconscious minds. This will also help you focus on your goal.

STEP 2 TAKE ACTION

No goal is any good without *action*!

Let me repeat that, no goal is any good without *action*! To succeed, you must take action to move toward your goal. To do this, you need two things:

1. Focus. You must be truly focused on just one goal for the next thirty days. You must think about it often. When you work toward it, you must do so with definite purpose. You must really want to accomplish it.

2. Time. You must spend at least one hour *every* day working toward your goal. You must do this *every day*, and you must truly dedicate that hour to achieving your goal. Remember seven hours in just one day each week does not equal one hour every day for a week. The consistency is critical.

STEP 3 ACHIEVE SUCCESS

If you have diligently followed the program for all thirty days, you will probably be amazed at the results. You may have achieved your goal before the thirty days were up. Whenever you have completed your goal, pick another goal and repeat the process. If you start with small goals and work up to bigger goals, then you will be increasing your confidence over time.

If you did not achieve your goal, determine why. Did you use the program properly? Did you pick a goal that was too big or a goal that was too difficult to do in thirty days? Once you have determined the reason, make the necessary changes and then do this exercise again for the next thirty days and see what happens.

I believe that this exercise is truly powerful. By focusing on just one goal and taking action toward it, you can accomplish it and then move to the next one. You must work toward goals like climbing a flight of stairs: by taking one step at a time.

It is also very enlightening to see how much you can achieve in such a short time.

The sky is the limit. If you do the exercises and put the challenge in this chapter into practice, then you should have a good beginning for a successful future.

Have a wonderful life!

P.S. I would like to hear from you and know how this book helped you. You can contact me on Facebook or LinkedIn or at www.BruceRaineSpeaker.com or at:

Bruce Raine
Seattle Arthro, Inc.
111 Deerwood Road, Suite 200
San Ramon, CA 94583

End Note

IT'S YOUR LIFE

You can get anything you want in life by Helping other people get what they want.
—Zig Ziglar

I hope that you have enjoyed learning the lessons in this book. My goal in life is to help people live fuller lives by teaching them what I have learned. I don't claim to be a guru or a wise man or anyone special. My only claim is that I have lived a dull boring life where I gave away all my power to others. I have also lived a fun, exciting life where I took control of my life, decided how I wanted to live it and then went out and enjoyed it.

You can accomplish anything you want in life. It is your life, live it the way that you desire.

Appendix A:

THE THREE PILLARS OF A SUCCESSFUL LIFE

I hope that you have enjoyed this book and even more important I hope that your life has changed because of it. I would like to leave you with a few thoughts. Here are what I consider to be the three most important ideas in the book:

There are three pillars that support a successful life. You must choose to develop these continually. You are never finished with any of the three, and you will use them simultaneously throughout your life.

PILLAR 1 ADD

ADD stands for "*Attitude Determines Destiny.*" Your attitude in life will determine how successful you will be. The best possible attitude is an *Attitude of Gratitude*.

PILLAR 2 GLUE

GLUE stands for "God Loves Us Eternally" or "God Loves U Eternally". I believe that the most important part of a successful life is a relationship with God that puts Him first and foremost in your life. This relationship provides you with values, guidance, and wisdom. It leads to success in all areas of life.

PILLAR 3 GAS

GAS stands for "Goals + *Action* = Success."

By using this process, you can achieve amazing results in a short period of time.

Appendix B:

THE ONLY LAWS WE NEED

I believe that there are too many laws today. The country would be better served by using just the Ten Commandments. If everyone followed them, there would be no crime, no wars, no family conflicts, etc. It would be easy to know what was right and wrong in any situation.

While it may not be easy to follow a set of laws, it is certainly easier if we choose the laws instead of having them thrust upon us. It is better if we understand the laws than having them so complicated that no one can understand them. It is better that we strive for perfection and fail than strive to avoid getting caught breaking a law that we don't understand or believe in.

Below are the Ten Commandments that I adapted from the book of Deuteronomy in the Bible and personalized. If you adopt these as your own personal code of conduct and try your best to live your life following these rules, then I firmly believe that you will be much more successful and happier in life.

THE TEN COMMANDMENTS

1 I shall have no other gods before God.

2 I shall not make for myself any idol.

3 I shall not take the name of the Lord in vain.

4 I shall observe the Sabbath day and keep it holy.

5 I shall honor my father and my mother.

6 I shall not murder.

7 I shall not commit adultery.

8 I shall not steal.

9 I shall not lie.

10 I shall not covet.

I believe that these are easy to understand. It may take you some time to understand fully the meaning of every one in minute detail but if you work at following these laws and work at better understanding them, then life will work like a wonderful dream. I know because when I started living my life in this manner my life improved in so many ways it thrills me every day.

ABOUT THE AUTHOR

Bruce Raine is a motivational speaker and author living in Pleasanton, California. He was born in Halifax, Nova Scotia, Canada. He moved to the San Francisco Bay Area and was a professor of accounting and computing at California State University in Hayward.

Personal growth has been a passion of his for the past thirty years and continues every day. With God at the center of his life and his passion for personal growth, he has achieved a level of contentment and peace in his life that he never dreamed possible.

This book was written to help anyone who suffered some type of trauma earlier in life. Bruce spent his childhood in the home of an alcoholic father and his adulthood in a series of unsuccessful relationships. With God's love and through counseling and personal growth he was able to deal with these past problems and find peace.

Bruce welcomes your comments and suggestions.

He also conducts seminars and workshops based upon the ideas in this book. Go to www.BruceRaineTaxes.com

COACHING

Two of Bruce's passions in life are teaching and encouraging others. Every day you can find him talking enthusiastically to someone telling them that they can do something that they think they can't do. If you would like to get his help to achieve your dreams, contact him at www.BruceRaineTaxes.com or 360-588-4239.

WRITING A BOOK:

> Everyone has a book in them just crying to get out. Writing a book is much easier than most people think. Bruce will walk you through the process and within one year or less you will have a book finished and for sale. Ask Bruce about his BONUS Program for when you finish your book.

BUILDING CONFIDENCE:

Few things scare people more than public speaking. However, it is a great asset in anyone's life. Public speaking builds confidence, gives you a skill that most people don't possess and makes you a leader amongst your peers. Bruce will walk you through the process and within one year or less you will be comfortable and confident giving a speech to a group of people. Ask Bruce about his BONUS Program for when you achieve your speaking goals.

For a 30-minute complementary consultation contact Bruce at www.BruceRaineTaxes.com

Book Bruce Raine

TO SPEAK AT YOUR NEXT EVENT

Do you want your next meeting to be meaningful to the attendees? Do you want them going home saying, "This was the best meeting that I ever attended!"? Then contact Bruce Raine and ask about having him as a workshop presenter for your next meeting.

Since 1977 Bruce has been speaking to audiences in Canada and the United States. He has more than 10,000 hours speaking in front of groups on a variety of topics. He will produce a custom message for your group that will inspire them to do greater things than they are currently doing. Bruce has a treasure trove of stories both humorous and meaningful which will entertain your group. They will be learning even though they may not realize it.

Bruce's philosophy is to use his boundless energy and passion to inspire his audience with stories. There is seldom a dull moment in one of Bruce's workshops.

Check out one of Bruce's workshop videos on his website www.BruceRaineSpeaker.com and see what he is like.

Contact Bruce for a complimentary pre-speech interview:
www.BruceRaineTaxes.com
360-588-4239

www.ingramcontent.com/pod-product-compliance
Lightning Source LLC
Chambersburg PA
CBHW060515170426
43199CB00011B/1454